GETTING HEALTHY
from the
INSIDE
OUT

GETTING HEALTHY *from the* INSIDE OUT

Harnessing the Power of
Belief, Mindset, and Faith

MICHAEL SCHÜLER

REAL PATH
PUBLISHING

Real Path Publishing
1001 S Main St, Ste 49
Kalispell, MT 59901
United States
www.realpathpublishing.com

ISBN: 979-8-9940317-0-4 (paperback)
ISBN: 979-8-9940317-3-5 (hardcover)
ISBN: 979-8-9940317-1-1 (eBook)

Library of Congress Control Number: 2026903726

Printed in the United States of America
First edition, 2026

To everyone who has ever Googled their symptoms and somehow ended up convinced they were either perfectly fine or had six months to live.

To those who followed the plan, took the supplement, did the workout, said the prayer, trusted the expert—and still wondered why their body didn't get the memo.

To anyone whose MRI, bloodwork, or diagnosis seemed to know them better than some of their friends.

This book is for the people who were told, *"You'll just have to live with it,"* and quietly thought, *"That can't be the whole story."*

It's for the faithful who love God but wish He came with clearer operating instructions. For the skeptics who love science but suspect it may be missing a chapter. And for anyone who has ever felt like their body was running outdated software… with no user manual.

As Hermes Trismegistus is often paraphrased, *"When the student is ready, the teacher appears."* Consider this book neither teacher nor cure—but a conversation. A nudge. A reminder that wisdom tends to show up once we stop interrupting it.

If something in these pages makes you laugh, pause, argue, or mutter, *"Well… that's uncomfortable,"* you're reading it correctly.

This book is dedicated to you—whole, healing, and far more intelligent than you've been led to believe.

CONTENTS

PART I: THE ROOTS OF HEALTH— MIND BEFORE BODY

Introduces the central premise that belief is the foundational blueprint of health. Blends neuroscience, scripture, Hermetic principles, and case studies showing how inner conviction becomes biological reality.

Explores psychoneuroimmunology, epigenetics, and neurotheology alongside biblical healing traditions. Shows how faith, emotion, and perception influence hormones, immunity, inflammation, and cellular repair.

Examines predictive coding, pain interpretation, identity-based perception, and resilience training. Includes military examples, personal recovery stories, and real testimonials demonstrating how perception drives healing outcomes.

PART II: THE SCIENCE OF BELIEF

Covers neuroplasticity, visualization, expectancy effects, and the biology of faith. Connects research to recovery and how belief-driven neural pathways accelerate healing.

PART III: THE SPIRITUAL DIMENSION

Presents a structured method for interpreting scripture through ancient context, spiritual symbolism, and modern health insights. Demonstrates how biblical narratives reveal psychological and biological healing principles.

PART IV: THE PRACTICE OF ALIGNMENT

Guides readers in constructing a personalized, sustainable framework combining belief, environment, lifestyle, relationships, and spiritual practice. Introduces the alignment ecosystem model.

My signature daily practice that integrates prayer, breathwork, visualization, gratitude, identity rehearsal, intention-setting, somatic awareness, and emotional coherence into one unified routine.

Deepens the alignment work with advanced belief-testing techniques. Incorporates my post-surgery recovery as a practical demonstration of faith under physical adversity and the triumph of identity-level healing.

PART V: THE PRACTICE OF BELIEVING

A transformative empowerment chapter showing how readers reclaim inner authority. Explains how belief, faith, identity, and agency activate the body's divine healing blueprint.

Addresses doubt, social pressure, family remarks, physical flare-ups, and contradictory "evidence." Teaches resilience, emotional mastery, spiritual warfare interpretation, and long-term alignment maintenance.

PREFACE

For most of my life, I believed what I was told about the body—that health was something managed by experts, prescribed through pills, and proven by scans.

After more than three decades of Army service, my medical records told a detailed story. X-rays, MRIs, CT scans, and clinical terminology documented every injury and limitation: traumatic brain injury, degenerative spine conditions, chronic pain, nerve damage, tinnitus, depression, anxiety, surgeries, and diagnoses that carried the weight of permanence.

The evidence was thorough. The pain was real. The conclusions felt final.

Doctors called it permanent. The system called it disability. I accepted it as truth.

At the time, that acceptance felt responsible—mature, even. After all, the scans didn't lie. But what I didn't yet understand was this: believing the evidence did not require becoming it.

Somewhere between the pain and the prescriptions, a question surfaced—one most of us are never taught to ask:

> What if the labels we accept quietly become the limits
> we live by?

I saw this pattern repeatedly—in conversations with loved ones, in my fitness studio, and in myself. People genuinely wanted to heal, yet defaulted to the belief that their bodies were fundamentally broken. A diagnosis stopped being information and became identity. From that moment on, every sensation reinforced the same story.

During my doctoral studies, I encountered research that disrupted that narrative. Not fringe theories, but work from respected scientists and physicians—often underemphasized rather than rejected—pointing to the same conclusion: the mind, emotions, and belief systems are not secondary to biology. They actively shape it.

Researchers such as Joe Dispenza, Ellen Langer, David Hamilton, Bruce Lipton, Lynne Zimmerman, and Gabor Maté—each from different disciplines—arrived at remarkably similar insights. Perception influences physiology. Chronic stress alters gene expression. Belief affects immune function, pain perception, and recovery.

At the same time, my study of Scripture and ancient wisdom revealed striking parallels.

"For as he thinketh in his heart, so is he"
PROVERBS 23:7, KJV

"And be not conformed to this world: but be ye transformed by the renewing of your mind."
ROMANS 12:2

And an ancient Hermetic principle expressed it succinctly:

"As within, so without."

What once sounded purely spiritual began to resemble principles of neuroplasticity and psychoneuroimmunology.

Gradually, I stopped identifying as disabled and began identifying as healing.

Through prayer, meditation, visualization, disciplined movement, and daily belief alignment, I observed steady change. Pain diminished. Function improved. Faith deepened beyond diagnosis. Healing did not arrive dramatically—but it arrived consistently.

This book is not an argument against medicine. It is an invitation to see health more completely.

This book is written for those who followed the plan, trusted the expert, took the supplement, said the prayer—and still sensed that something essential was missing. It is for the faithful who love God but have quietly struggled to reconcile belief with biology. And it is for the skeptics who trust science yet suspect it may not tell the whole story.

This book does not ask you to choose between faith and science. It invites you to see how they converge—how belief becomes biology, how prayer becomes physiology, and how healing emerges when mind, body, and spirit move in alignment. If you are willing to examine not only what you believe, but how deeply you believe it, the path forward may be closer—and more personal—than you ever imagined.

WHY THIS BOOK EXISTS

We live in an age of extraordinary medical knowledge. Never before have we had such access to health information, advanced diagnostics, pharmaceuticals, and expert guidance. And yet, despite this unprecedented progress, chronic illness, anxiety, autoimmune disease, depression, and dependence on medication continue to rise at alarming rates.

This contradiction raises an uncomfortable question: If we know more about health than ever before, why are so many people still unwell?

The answer explored in this book is both simple and disruptive. Health is not determined primarily by information, technology, or even biology. It is shaped—often unconsciously—by belief.

Modern science increasingly confirms what ancient wisdom has long suggested: the mind does not merely influence the body; it actively participates in shaping it. Thoughts, expectations, emotional patterns, and deeply held assumptions continuously signal the nervous system, regulate hormones, influence immune function, and even affect gene expression. In other words, biology responds to perception.

Yet most approaches to health focus almost exclusively on the external—symptoms, measurements, diagnoses, and interventions—while overlooking the internal environment in which healing either unfolds or stalls. When belief remains misaligned, even the most sophisticated treatments often provide only temporary relief.

Getting Healthy from the Inside Out is written to address this missing dimension.

Drawing from neuroscience, epigenetics, psychology, lifestyle medicine, theology, and ancient spiritual traditions, this book presents a unified framework for understanding health as a process of alignment. It shows how the integration of mind, body, and spirit creates the conditions in which healing becomes possible—and sustainable.

This is not a rejection of medicine or scientific progress. It is an expansion of the model. Medicine excels at managing acute conditions and diagnosing structural problems. But lasting health often requires something deeper: a shift in identity, perception, and the beliefs we hold about our bodies, our limits, and what is possible.

Throughout this book, you will encounter research, case studies, personal experiences, and spiritual insights that point to the same conclusion: the body is not broken, passive, or separate from consciousness. It is responsive, adaptive, and designed to heal when supported by coherent belief, emotional regulation, and meaning.

The central claim of this work is straightforward: When belief aligns with biological truth and spiritual identity, the body responds.

Healing, then, is not a mysterious anomaly or a rare miracle. It is a natural outcome of alignment—one that becomes increasingly accessible as we learn to listen inward, question inherited narratives, and reclaim responsibility for our own well-being.

This book exists for those who sense that health is more than management, more than maintenance, and more than medication. It is for those ready to explore healing not as something done *to* them, but as a process that begins *within* them.

What follows is not a promise of instant cures, but an invitation: to rethink health, to reconsider belief, and to rediscover the innate intelligence already working inside you.

THE PARADOX OF MODERN HEALTH

We live in a time of extraordinary medical capability. We can map the brain in real time, sequence the genome, replace joints, regulate hormones, and suppress symptoms with remarkable precision. Health information is abundant—apps, wearables, podcasts, protocols, specialists, and endless advice available at the tap of a screen.

And yet, something is not working.

Rates of chronic illness continue to rise. Anxiety and depression are increasingly common. Autoimmune conditions, metabolic disease, persistent pain, and dependence on medication have become normalized. Many people are doing "everything right" and still feel unwell—physically, emotionally, or both.

This is the paradox of modern health: the more we know, the less whole we seem to feel.

For many, health has become an endless cycle of management rather than a movement toward restoration. We track symptoms, adjust treatments, and monitor markers—often without ever addressing the deeper question beneath it all: *What internal environment is the body responding to?*

Most models of health focus outward—on what can be measured, labeled, corrected, or controlled. These tools are valuable, but incomplete. They often overlook the inner dimension where healing either begins or quietly stalls: belief.

Not belief as optimism or denial. Belief as the set of assumptions—conscious and unconscious—that shape perception, identity, expectation, and meaning.

Modern neuroscience now understands that the brain does not passively receive reality; it predicts it. Biology does not merely react to the world; it responds to interpretation. Hormones, immune cells, inflammatory pathways, and even gene expression are influenced by how safety, threat, hope, and possibility are internally perceived.

In other words, the body is listening.

This does not mean illness is imagined, nor does it imply blame. Pain is real. Disease is real. Diagnosis matters. But the story does not end there. Increasingly, research suggests that *how we understand our bodies* becomes part of the biological signal they follow.

Yet few people are ever taught what to do with this insight.

We are given instructions for compliance, not coherence. We are told what is wrong, rarely what is possible. We learn how to manage conditions, but not how to participate consciously in healing. Over time, a diagnosis can quietly shift from being useful information to becoming an identity—and once that happens, every sensation reinforces the same conclusion.

This book exists because that conclusion is incomplete.

Across neuroscience, epigenetics, psychology, lifestyle medicine, and even theology, a more integrated picture is emerging—one that sees health not as a mechanical outcome, but as a dynamic relationship between mind, body, and spirit. When these systems align, the body often does what it was designed to do: adapt, repair, and recover.

Ancient traditions understood this intuitively. Scripture speaks of transformation through renewal of the mind. Hermetic teachings point to the inner world as the source of the outer. These were not metaphors meant to replace the physical—they were insights into how reality operates.

Today, science is beginning to catch up.

The chapters that follow do not ask you to reject medicine, deny symptoms, or abandon reason. They ask you to expand the framework—to include belief as a biological force, meaning as a physiological signal, and identity as a powerful determinant of health.

This is not a book about quick fixes or guaranteed outcomes. It is about learning how to create the internal conditions in which healing becomes more likely, more sustainable, and more aligned with who you are.

You do not need to accept everything here immediately. You do not need to agree with every conclusion. All that is required is a willingness to consider a different starting point—one that places authority not solely in external systems, but also within your own lived experience.

If you have ever felt frustrated by treatments that managed symptoms but never addressed the whole of you… If you have sensed that health is more than compliance and chemistry… If you are ready to explore healing not as something done *to* you, but as a process that begins *within* you…

Then this book is written for you.

What follows is an invitation—not to believe blindly, but to listen more deeply. To question inherited narratives. To reconnect with the intelligence already at work inside your body.

The journey ahead is not about becoming someone new. It is about remembering what has always been there.

HOW TO READ
THIS BOOK

This book brings together perspectives that are often kept separate: modern science and ancient wisdom, medical research and lived experience, faith and physiology. Because of that, readers will arrive with different assumptions—and that's not only expected, it's welcome.

If you approach this book primarily from a scientific or medical background, you may encounter language drawn from spirituality, Scripture, or inner experience that feels unfamiliar. You are not being asked to suspend reason or abandon evidence. You are invited to consider how emerging research in neuroscience, psychology, and epigenetics increasingly points to the same conclusions that spiritual traditions articulated long before we had imaging machines and laboratories.

If you approach this book from a faith-based or spiritual background, you may encounter research findings, biological mechanisms, and psychological frameworks that feel technical or overly analytical. You are not being asked to replace faith with science. You are invited to see how scientific discovery can illuminate—and often affirm—the wisdom already present in Scripture and spiritual practice.

This book is not meant to be read defensively.

You do not need to agree with every idea to benefit from the whole. You do not need to adopt new beliefs immediately. You are encouraged to notice what resonates, question what doesn't, and remain open to how understanding evolves over time.

Some chapters are explanatory. Others are reflective. Some invite intellectual engagement, while others invite practice. You may find yourself returning to certain sections more than others—that is part of the process.

Most importantly, this book is not about denying illness, dismissing medicine, or blaming individuals for their health challenges. Pain is real. Diagnosis matters. Medical care saves lives. The perspective offered here simply expands the conversation by including the internal environment—belief, perception, emotion, meaning—as legitimate contributors to health and healing.

Think of this book as a guide rather than a prescription.

Read it slowly. Reflect honestly. Apply gently. Pay attention not only to what you think, but to how your body responds as you read. Healing, as explored here, is not a single insight or technique—it is a relationship that unfolds over time.

Above all, allow this book to meet you where you are. Whether skeptical or faithful, analytical or intuitive, the journey ahead begins with curiosity and a willingness to listen—both outwardly and within.

PART I

THE ROOTS OF HEALTH—MIND BEFORE BODY

CHAPTER 1

THE HIDDEN BLUEPRINT

Belief Shapes Biology

"According to your faith be it unto you."
MATTHEW 9:29

THE HIDDEN BLUEPRINT—
BELIEF SHAPES BIOLOGY

Most people think of health as something physical—a product of diet, exercise, or genetics. We grow up believing the body operates like a machine: when a part breaks, it is repaired or replaced. But the human body is not a machine. It is a living, adaptive system—governed not only by chemistry, but by consciousness.

Every thought you think, every belief you hold, and every emotion you feel sends biochemical signals throughout your body. These signals influence the nervous system, regulate immune response, and even affect gene expression. Modern neuroscience now confirms what ancient Scripture and mystic traditions have long suggested: the mind is not confined to the brain—it is embodied (Dispenza, 2014; Lipton, 2005).

THE SCIENCE OF THOUGHT AS MEDICINE

In *The Biology of Belief*, Dr. Bruce Lipton demonstrated that perception—what we believe to be true—can influence how genes express themselves. This field, known as epigenetics, shows that genes are not fixed instructions but responsive systems, continually adapting to the chemical and energetic environment shaped by thought and emotion (Lipton, 2005).

When we experience fear, the brain releases stress hormones such as cortisol and adrenaline, signaling the body to prepare for threat. When this response becomes chronic, it contributes to inflammation, immune suppression, and accelerated cellular wear. By contrast, states such as gratitude, joy, and faith stimulate the release of oxytocin, serotonin, and endorphins—biochemical signals associated with repair, resilience, and healing (Hamilton, 2018).

In *How Your Mind Can Heal Your Body*, Dr. David Hamilton documents studies in which patients experienced measurable recovery through visualization alone. In one notable case, stroke patients who mentally rehearsed hand movements regained function more rapidly than those relying on physical therapy alone. The brain, it appears, responds to vividly imagined experience in much the same way it responds to physical action.

BELIEF AND THE BODY ELECTRIC

Thought does not operate only through chemistry; it also generates measurable electrical and magnetic activity. Research from the HeartMath Institute shows that the heart produces the largest electromagnetic field in the human body, extending beyond the skin. When emotions such as appreciation or love are sustained, this field becomes more coherent, influencing internal physiology and interpersonal interaction alike (HeartMath Institute, 2017).

Scripture expresses this principle poetically:

"For the life of the flesh is in the blood."
LEVITICUS 17:11, KJV

Biblical language points to an unseen source animating physical life—an ordering intelligence beneath the visible form.

CASE STUDY: THE VETERAN WHO FORGOT TO BE SICK

Consider a fellow soldier I'll call Anthony. After years of chronic back pain, migraines, and PTSD symptoms, he enrolled in a neurofeedback study focused on mindfulness and visualization. Over six months, his daily pain levels dropped from consistent eights to occasional twos.

When asked what had changed most, he answered simply, "I stopped identifying as broken."

That shift—from victim to whole—initiated new neural pathways. MRI scans later confirmed structural changes in his anterior cingulate cortex, a region associated with emotional regulation and pain modulation. His healing began not with a new treatment, but with a new belief.

RESILIENCE AND THE CHOICE TO BE WHOLE

That realization mirrored my own experience after retiring from the Army. I carried the same aches, scars, and surgical reminders of long service—but I made a deliberate decision not to wear the identity of disabled.

During my time in uniform, I was exposed to the Army's **Master Resilience Training (MRT)**—a program designed to teach soldiers how to train mindset, regulate emotion, and maintain effectiveness under sustained stress.

What stayed with me was not the program itself, but the discovery it revealed: inner orientation could be deliberately shaped—and the body responded accordingly. The same discipline we applied to mission success could be applied inward, to the mission of healing. The battlefield was no longer external; it was within consciousness itself.

Resilience, I learned, is not about enduring pain. It is about transforming its meaning. When I stopped identifying as broken, my body responded as if it had received new instructions. Healing was not immediate—but it began the moment belief shifted.

BELIEF IN SCRIPTURE AND HERMETICS

The Gospel of Matthew records Jesus saying,

"According to your faith be it unto you." (*Matthew 9:29*)

This is not merely moral encouragement; it reflects a metaphysical principle. Hermetic philosophy echoes the same truth. *The Kybalion* teaches:

> *"The All is Mind; the Universe is Mental."*
> **THE KYBALION, 1908/2011**

Both traditions affirm the same insight: the inner world shapes the outer world.

When belief aligns with divine design—the understanding that the human body is created with intelligence and order—it activates systems of regeneration and coherence. Modern psychoneuroimmunology supports this relationship, showing that faith, hope, and inner peace correlate with reduced cortisol, improved immune markers, and faster recovery rates (Koenig, 2012).

FROM KNOWING TO EMBODYING

Most people intellectually accept that mindset matters. Far fewer embody that truth. We consume books, podcasts, and sermons, yet still place more trust in diagnosis than in design.

To bridge that gap, belief must move from concept to experience—from something we know to something we feel as real. Dr. Joe Dispenza teaches that healing occurs when elevated emotion and clear intention synchronize within the body. This is the moment belief becomes biology. When mind, heart, and physiology operate in coherence, new possibilities emerge—possibilities Western medicine is only beginning to explain (Dispenza, 2019).

REFLECTION

Healing begins not by fixing the body, but by renewing the mind. You are not a victim of your biology—you are an active participant in shaping it.

The blueprint has always been within you, waiting to be redrawn by belief.

CHAPTER 2

THE MIND-BODY CONNECTION

Science and Scripture

*Keep thy heart with all diligence; for
out of it are the issues of life."*
PROVERBS 4:23

In the last century, medicine became a discipline of parts. The mind belonged to psychology, the body to biology, and the soul—if acknowledged at all—to theology. Yet human beings do not live divided. Every thought alters chemistry. Every emotion carries a molecular signature. Every belief, prayer, or fear reverberates through hormone, nerve, and gene.

The frontier of modern science is now confirming what ancient Scripture implied all along: the body reflects the state of the mind.

Long before laboratories could measure neurotransmitters or cortisol, contemplative traditions across cultures observed something similar through direct experience. Suffering intensified not simply because pain existed, but because the mind resisted what was happening. When resistance became habitual, the body carried the burden.

THE BIOLOGY OF BELIEF

The emergence of psychoneuroimmunology revealed that the brain, nervous system, and immune system communicate through a shared biochemical language. Neurotransmitters once thought to operate exclusively in the brain were found on immune cells, demonstrating that thought and immunity are biologically intertwined (Pert, 1997).

Stress hormones such as cortisol suppress cellular repair and immune coordination, while emotional states associated with gratitude, compassion, and safety enhance cellular communication and resilience. These responses are not symbolic; they are measurable and repeatable.

Dr. Bruce Lipton expanded this understanding through epigenetics—the study of how perception and environment influence gene expression. Genes, he demonstrated, are not rigid determinants but responsive systems. When a person perceives safety, connection, and purpose, the body shifts into growth and repair. When fear and chronic stress dominate, defense takes priority and healing slows (Lipton, 2015).

In this light, belief is not metaphorical. It is biological instruction.

Dr. David Hamilton documented similar effects, showing that positive expectation activates neurochemical cascades comparable to pharmacological interventions (Hamilton, 2018). Other studies have demonstrated that consistent mental and emotional training influences gene expression related to inflammation, pain perception, and mood regulation (Zimmerman, 2020).

Thought and emotion, then, are not abstract experiences. They are physiological forces.

THE SOLDIER'S LESSON: RESILIENCE AS BIOLOGY

What mattered most was not the Master Resilience Training itself, but what it revealed under pressure. We learned—sometimes the hard way—that perception was not passive. It could be trained, redirected, and stabilized in real time.

Under stress, we practiced observing thought patterns, regulating emotional responses, and reframing adversity as challenge rather than threat. When perception shifted, physiology followed. Heart rate steadied. Focus sharpened. Recovery improved. The body responded to meaning before it ever responded to circumstance.

Only later did I recognize this for what it was: applied mind-body science. Belief was not being discussed philosophically; it was being exercised operationally.

We didn't call it neuroscience at the time—we called it staying functional.

SCRIPTURE AND THE PHYSIOLOGY OF THOUGHT

Scripture articulates this integration with remarkable clarity:

"For as he thinketh in his heart, so is he."
PROVERBS 23:7, KJV

In Hebrew, the word *lev* ("heart") refers not only to emotion, but to will, intention, and consciousness. Scripture does not separate psychology from physiology; it views the human being as an integrated unity.

Paul reinforces this understanding:

> *"And be not conformed to this world: but be ye*
> *transformed by the renewing of your mind."*
> **ROMANS 12:2**

The Greek *metamorphoō* refers to a change of form. Modern science now demonstrates that mental renewal produces measurable biological effects. Meditation alters gene expression associated with inflammation, while prayer modulates heart-rate variability and immune function (Kaliman et al., 2014; Koenig, 2012).

Even Christ's healings often begin with belief:

> *"Thy faith hath made thee whole."*
> **MARK 5:34**

Faith—aligned conviction, emotion, and expectation—creates coherence between mind and body. When belief shifts toward wholeness, the physiology of repair follows.

THE NEUROTHEOLOGY OF HEALING

Neurotheology examines how spiritual practice shapes the brain. Research shows that sustained prayer and meditation increase activity in the prefrontal cortex—associated with focus, compassion, and regulation—while quieting the amygdala, the brain's primary fear center (Newberg, 2018).

The result is improved emotional regulation and reduced stress chemistry. Studies from the HeartMath Institute similarly demonstrate that sustained feelings of gratitude or love synchronize heart and brain rhythms, producing coherent electrical patterns associated with enhanced immune response and cognitive clarity (McCraty et al., 2009). Scripture describes this embodied harmony as *shalom*—integrated peace within body, mind, and spirit.

CASE STUDY: SARAH AND THE SHIFT OF BELIEF

Sarah, a forty-two-year-old mother of three, spent years struggling with chronic fatigue. Extensive testing revealed no clear pathology, yet her exhaustion persisted. Her turning point came not through medication, but through identity work.

With therapeutic support, she began rewriting her internal narrative—from "I am sick" to "I am healing." Within months, her energy improved, inflammatory markers normalized, and her mood stabilized.

When subconscious identity shifts from victim to participant in healing, biology reorganizes accordingly. This is not placebo. It is the body responding to new internal signals (Zimmerman, 2020).

BRIDGING THE DIVIDE

Western medicine often treats the mind as software and the body as hardware, loosely connected by metaphor. Yet both science and Scripture point to a single operating system: consciousness.

What we habitually think, feel, and attend to writes the code governing physiological function. Healing, therefore, is not only about changing behavior—it is about renewing awareness.

When scientific understanding meets spiritual wisdom, the false divide between medicine and faith dissolves. Health ceases to be something we pursue externally and becomes something we remember internally.

CHAPTER 3

PERCEPTION AND REALITY

How the Brain Filters Health

"The light of the body is the eye…"
MATTHEW 6:22

Our senses do not record reality; they interpret it. Neuroscientists estimate that the human brain processes roughly eleven million bits of information per second, yet conscious awareness registers fewer than fifty (Zimmerman, 2020). Everything else is filtered automatically through expectation, memory, and belief.

In matters of health, this filtering process determines what we notice—and what we amplify. A person who believes the body is fragile unconsciously scans for pain and fatigue, reinforcing both. By contrast, one who perceives the body as resilient is more likely to notice capacity, recovery, and strength even in discomfort.

Dr. David Hamilton explains that the placebo effect is not deception, but demonstration. When we believe healing is occurring, the brain releases real biochemicals—endorphins, dopamine, and oxytocin—that generate measurable improvement. The body follows the map the mind provides (Hamilton, 2018).

Neuroscientist Lisa Feldman Barrett adds that emotions are not reactions to reality, but predictions generated by the brain based on past experience. When perception changes, emotional response changes. And when emotion changes, physiology follows (Barrett, 2017).

BIBLICAL FOUNDATIONS OF PERCEPTION

Scripture frames perception as both spiritual lens and responsibility.

> *"The light of the body is the eye: if therefore thine eye*
> *be single, thy whole body shall be full of light."*
> **MATTHEW 6:22, KJV**

In Hebraic thought, the "eye" signifies not merely vision, but understanding. Clear perception fills the whole being with vitality; distorted perception diminishes both spirit and body.

Paul echoes this orientation:

> *"While we look not at the things which are*
> *seen, but at the things which are not seen."*
> **2 CORINTHIANS 4:18**

Scripture repeatedly points beyond surface appearances, insisting that reality is shaped first in consciousness before it manifests in form.

Hermetic philosophy captures the same insight succinctly: *as within, so without* (*The Kybalion*). This echoes Proverbs 23:7's declaration that inner orientation shapes lived experience.

NEUROSCIENCE OF FOCUS AND HEALING

Neuroimaging research demonstrates that sustained prayer or meditation focused on love or gratitude quiets the amygdala—the brain's threat-detection center—while increasing activity in the prefrontal cortex, the region responsible for clarity, compassion, and executive control (Newberg, 2018).

Repeated focus reshapes neural architecture through neuroplasticity. What we consistently attend to becomes structurally embedded in the brain (Siegel, 2010).

At the cellular level, research shows that perception—not DNA—directs cellular behavior. Fear-based perception triggers stress hormones that restrict growth and repair, while perceptions rooted in safety and connection open pathways for nourishment and regeneration (Lipton, 2015).

Perception, then, is not metaphorical. It is molecular.

PERSONAL REFLECTION:
LEARNING TO SEE DIFFERENTLY

When I left the Army, I carried not only physical pain, but an invisible lens of limitation. My medical records—stacked thick with evidence—appeared to define who I was: damaged, disabled, and diminished.

But belief, as I came to understand through study and spiritual practice, was never meant to be outsourced to documentation.

Drawing on the resilience principles I once taught, I began retraining perception. Instead of scanning for pain, I scanned for capacity. Instead of identifying as injured, I practiced identifying as healing.

Over time, my body responded. Inflammation decreased. Recovery accelerated. Rest deepened. I had not altered anatomy—I had altered attention.

Paul's instruction reads less like encouragement and more like instruction:

> *"Whatsoever things are true, whatsoever things*
> *are honest, whatsoever things are just, whatsoever*
> *things are pure… think on these things."*
> **PHILIPPIANS 4:8**

The nervous system, it turns out, is less interested in our diagnoses than our habits of attention.

CASE STUDY: THE VISION OF HEALING

A study published in *Psychosomatic Medicine* examined the role of expectation in pain management. Patients told a topical cream would relieve pain experienced a seventy percent reduction in discomfort—despite receiving a placebo. Brain imaging revealed changes in regions central to pain modulation (Crichton et al., 2015).

Belief functioned as pharmacology.

Similar outcomes appear when visualization is paired with emotional engagement. When imagery is accompanied by gratitude or faith, measurable biological changes follow. Visualization, when embodied, becomes instruction to the body (Hamilton, 2018).

In the Gospels, Jesus often begins healing encounters with a perceptual inquiry:

> *"Believe ye that I am able to do this?"*
> **MATTHEW 9:28**

Seeing differently preceded being differently.

MYSTIC PARALLEL: THE INNER EYE

Hermetic tradition teaches that reality mirrors consciousness:

"The All is Mind; the Universe is Mental."
THE KYBALION, 1908/2011

Scripture expresses the same truth in prayer:

"Open thou mine eyes, that I may behold
wondrous things out of thy law."
PSALM 119:18

Across mystical traditions, perception is understood not as observation alone, but as participation. To see rightly is to align awareness with divine order.

INTEGRATING SCIENCE, SCRIPTURE, AND SELF

Neuroscience, Scripture, and mysticism converge on a shared truth: what we perceive determines what we receive. Mind and body operate not in hierarchy, but in harmony.

Healing begins with purified perception—seeing oneself not as a diagnosis, but as a design still unfolding.

Scripture names this higher vision plainly:

"For we walk by faith, not by sight."
2 CORINTHIANS 5:7

Faith, then, is not blindness. It is deeper perception.

PART II

THE SCIENCE OF BELIEF

CHAPTER 4

THE NEUROSCIENCE OF FAITH AND EXPECTATION

"And be not conformed to this world: but be ye transformed by the renewing of your mind."

ROMANS 12:2

THE BRAIN AS THE DIRECTOR OF HEALING

If the body is the theater of health, the brain is its director. Every cell, organ, and physiological process responds to neural instruction. Transformation—whether spiritual or physical—begins when those instructions change.

For much of modern history, medicine treated the brain as fixed hardware, governed largely by genetics and resistant to change. The discovery of neuroplasticity overturned that assumption. The adult brain is not static; it continuously rewires itself in response to learning, attention, emotion, and belief (Doidge, 2007).

Paul's insight—that transformation begins with the renewal of the mind—describes in theological language what neuroscience now observes at the synaptic level.

NEUROPLASTICITY— THE BRAIN'S CAPACITY TO REWIRE

Neuroplasticity governs not only learning, but the body's ability to regulate, adapt, and repair itself. Research shows that imagining movement activates many of the same neural circuits as performing the movement physically (Decety, 1996). Visualization, therefore, is not fantasy—it is neural rehearsal.

I encountered this principle firsthand following ACL-replacement surgery. Despite diligent physical therapy, my progress plateaued. My therapist eventually explained that the limitation was no longer in the knee itself, but in the communication between brain and muscle. The nervous system was still protecting the injury.

When I began intentionally visualizing movement—seeing flexibility rather than pain—progress resumed. Range of motion improved not because tissue changed overnight, but because the brain updated its expectations. Belief altered instruction.

Not long afterward, I completed the Marine Corps Marathon—not as an act of force, but as evidence that the brain had released the body to move again.

BELIEF AND EXPECTATION SHAPE PHYSIOLOGY

Modern neuroscience increasingly confirms what Scripture has long declared: belief functions as biological command.

Placebo research demonstrates that expectation alone can activate genuine healing pathways (Benedetti et al., 2005). Remarkably, studies show that improvement can occur even when individuals know they are receiving a placebo (Kaptchuk et al., 2010). Expectation modulates neurochemistry—altering dopamine, serotonin, endorphins, and cortisol.

The inverse phenomenon, known as the nocebo effect, reveals the cost of negative expectation. Fear-based beliefs amplify pain, inflammation, and physiological distress (Hahn, 1997).

Scripture expresses this principle succinctly:

> *"For as he thinketh in his heart, so is he."*
> **PROVERBS 23:7, KJV**

The subconscious—shaped by repetition, emotion, and identity—teaches the body what to anticipate. To change physiology, the internal narrative must change.

THE BRAIN–BODY PATHWAYS OF BELIEF

One of the primary conduits between thought and physiology is the vagus nerve—a major communication pathway linking brain, heart, lungs, and digestive organs. Emotional states such as fear, gratitude, or trust send distinct signals through this network, influencing heart rate, immune response, and inflammation (Pert, 1997; Siegel, 2010).

Fear activates the sympathetic fight-or-flight response. Gratitude and trust activate the parasympathetic rest-and-repair system.

Neuroimaging studies show that meditation and prayer increase activity in the prefrontal cortex—associated with focus, compassion, and self-regulation—while quieting the amygdala, the brain's threat-detection center (Newberg, 2018). This shift promotes heart–brain coherence, synchronizing rhythms that support emotional stability and physiological resilience (McCraty et al., 2009).

In the language of Scripture, this embodied harmony is called *shalom*—peace made flesh.

THE POWER OF EXPECTATION—
FAITH AS PHARMACOLOGY

The placebo effect reveals a profound truth: belief itself acts as medicine.

During World War II, anesthesiologist Henry Beecher administered saline injections to wounded soldiers while telling them it was morphine. Pain subsided. Vital signs stabilized. This observation launched modern placebo research, later confirmed through brain imaging showing that placebo-induced relief activates the same neural pathways as opioid medication (Beecher, 1955; Benedetti, 2014).

David Hamilton summarizes the insight plainly:

> *"The body does not distinguish between a powerful belief*
> *and a powerful drug—it responds to expectation."*
> HAMILTON, 2018

In the language of faith, Jesus expressed the same principle:

> *"According to your faith be it unto you."*
> MATTHEW 9:29

Both statements describe the same biological law: the body organizes itself around what the mind expects to be true.

THE NEUROTHEOLOGY
OF FAITH AND FOCUS

Sustained prayer, meditation, and contemplative practice produce measurable structural changes in the brain. Research shows that regular spiritual engagement strengthens regions associated with executive control and emotional regulation while dampening fear circuitry (Newberg, 2018).

Studies of heart–brain coherence further demonstrate that emotions such as gratitude and compassion synchronize neural and cardiovascular rhythms into stable, efficient patterns linked to immune balance and cognitive clarity (McCraty et al., 2009).

Scripture names this alignment symbolically:

> *"The light of the body is the eye: if therefore thine eye*
> *be single, thy whole body shall be full of light."*
> **MATTHEW 6:22**

Faith, then, is not superstition. It is neurobiological alignment with order.

MODERN DISCOVERIES: MINDFULNESS, GENES, AND HEALING

Recent research continues to validate these principles at the molecular level. Mindfulness practices downregulate inflammatory gene expression, while brain-imaging studies show improved neural connectivity and coherence (Creswell et al., 2022; Gotink et al., 2023). Heart-rate-variability research further links emotional regulation with cognitive performance and stress resilience (Gupta et al., 2024).

Viewed through epigenetics, the internal environment of thought and emotion determines which genes are activated or silenced (Lipton, 2015). Peace, faith, and focused attention are not abstractions. They are biological events.

REFLECTION

Faith and expectation are not passive attitudes. They are active forces shaping neural circuitry, hormonal balance, immune response, and cellular behavior.

When the mind is renewed, the body reorganizes.

Belief, consistently practiced, becomes instruction. Expectation, sustained, becomes biology.

CHAPTER 5

EPIGENETICS AND LIFESTYLE MEDICINE

"What? know ye not that your body is the temple
of the Holy Ghost which is in you, which ye
have of God, and ye are not your own?"
1 CORINTHIANS 6:19

THE NEW BIOLOGY OF CHOICE

For much of the twentieth century, genes were treated as destiny. If heart disease, diabetes, depression, or addiction ran in your family, those outcomes were often assumed to be inevitable—an inherited script written in DNA.

Modern science has rewritten that story.

Epigenetics reveals that genes are not fixed instructions but responsive systems, continually shaped by lifestyle, emotion, environment, and belief. DNA provides the blueprint, but experience determines how that blueprint is read.

What we eat, how we move, how we sleep, how we think, and what we believe all send molecular signals that influence genetic expression. The human genome is less a machine than an instrument—awaiting the consciousness that plays it.

Bruce Lipton summarized this shift plainly:

> *"Genes are not the source of our destiny; they
> are the result of our perceptions."*
> **LIPTON, 2015**

Our biology listens.

GENES AS RESPONSIVE INSTRUMENTS

Lipton's early experiments demonstrated that the environment surrounding a cell—its chemical and energetic context—determines how genes behave. A healthy cell placed in a toxic environment becomes diseased. A stressed cell placed in a nurturing environment begins to recover.

The same principle governs the human body. Our internal environment—thoughts, emotions, expectations, and meaning—functions as the cellular ecosystem in which health either flourishes or falters.

A landmark study by Meaney and Szyf showed that nurturing behavior altered the genetic expression of stress-response hormones in offspring. These changes persisted into adulthood and were passed to subsequent generations (Meaney & Szyf, 2005). Love and safety leave biological traces—just as fear and neglect do.

Scripture names this principle succinctly:

> *"Be not deceived; God is not mocked: for whatsoever
> a man soweth, that shall he also reap."*
> **GALATIANS 6:7, KJV**

What we sow internally takes root at the molecular level.

LIFESTYLE AS GENE MODULATOR

If genes are instruments, lifestyle is the music we play.

Lifestyle medicine integrates movement, nutrition, sleep, stress regulation, and relational support—not merely to manage symptoms, but to influence genetic expression itself.

Dean Ornish demonstrated that comprehensive lifestyle changes—including nutrition, movement, stress reduction, and social connection—increased telomerase activity, slowing markers of biological aging (Ornish, 2008). Elizabeth Blackburn and Elissa Epel further showed that lifestyle and mindset directly influence telomere length (Blackburn & Epel, 2017). In measurable terms, hope extends life.

Nutrition communicates directly with our genes. Diets rich in antioxidants and omega-3 fatty acids activate pathways associated with repair and longevity, while highly processed foods and chronic stress amplify inflammation and degeneration.

Mindset amplifies every input. Movement performed with joy produces a different hormonal signature than movement driven by guilt or fear. Every choice is a biochemical conversation.

STRESS, TRAUMA, AND EPIGENETIC IMPRINTS

Stress is not merely psychological; it is epigenetic messaging.

Chronic fear triggers sustained release of cortisol and adrenaline, signaling genes associated with inflammation, metabolic dysfunction, and immune suppression. Over time, these signals leave epigenetic imprints—particularly in those exposed to early-life trauma.

The Adverse Childhood Experiences studies revealed that childhood stress dramatically increases the risk of adult chronic illness, depression, and cardiovascular disease (Shonkoff et al., 2012). Trauma writes itself into biology.

Yet these marks are not permanent.

Practices such as meditation, prayer, forgiveness, and gratitude downregulate pro-inflammatory gene expression and restore immune balance (Kaliman et al., 2014; Bhasin et al., 2013).

In the language of faith, this is redemption at the cellular level.

BELIEF AND LIFESTYLE SYNERGY

Genes do not respond only to physical inputs; they respond to meaning.

Two people may follow identical diets or exercise routines yet experience different outcomes. Often, the difference lies not in compliance, but in belief and emotional coherence.

When movement is infused with joy or gratitude, it becomes an act of creation rather than correction. Scripture captures this integration:

> *"For in him we live, and move, and have our being."*
> ACTS 17:28

To view the body as a temple is to approach lifestyle not as maintenance, but as worship. Discipline becomes devotion. Health becomes harmony.

THE SPIRIT-SCIENCE BRIDGE

The ancient axiom *as within, so without* finds tangible expression in epigenetics. The outer body reflects the inner world.

Research now confirms that compassion, meditation, and faith-based gratitude influence DNA methylation patterns related to stress and immunity. When peace becomes the internal state, cells learn peace.

Here, theology and biology converge: the image of God expressed through living tissue.

PERSONAL REFLECTION— REWRITING THE SCRIPT

As I applied these principles in my own life, I began to see that many of my perceived genetic limitations were inherited beliefs more than inherited biology. My family medical history told one story. My faith told another.

When I began living with intention—choosing food prayerfully, movement mindfully, and rest without guilt—my physiology responded. The same body that once expressed pain began to express peace.

My DNA did not change. The message I sent to it did.

We do not need to battle our biology. We need to lead it.

PRACTICAL STEPS TO ACTIVATE HEALING GENES

- **Movement with Intention:** Move with mindful focus. Visualize vitality with every motion.

- **Nutrition as Communication:** Eat whole, living foods. Offer gratitude before meals.

- **Stress Reversal through Stillness:** Practice prayer, meditation, or slow breathing to shift the body from defense to repair.

- **Sacred Rest:** Prioritize consistent, restorative sleep. Cellular renewal peaks during rest.

- **Belief Alignment:** Anchor each habit in faith and gratitude. Expect cooperation from your body.

These are not acts of willpower.
They are acts of stewardship.

CLOSING INSIGHT

Epigenetics reveals a divine partnership: we are not prisoners of our DNA, but stewards of it. What we believe, how we love, and how we live write the story our genes tell.

When belief directs behavior and behavior aligns with love, the genome sings the song of wholeness.

CHAPTER 6

THE FOUR PILLARS OF HUMAN HEALTH

What the Research Really Shows

"I am fearfully and wonderfully made."
PSALM 139:14

For decades, health was framed as a simple equation: eat well, move more, sleep enough. While these behaviors matter, this model overlooked the most influential variable of all—the internal environment.

Today, neuroscience, psychoneuroimmunology, and epigenetics reveal a more comprehensive picture. Beliefs, emotions, mindset, and perception influence biology as powerfully as—sometimes more than—diet or exercise alone.

Across population studies, clinical trials, and molecular research, four domains consistently emerge as the primary drivers of long-term health outcomes: mental and emotional state, diet, sleep, and movement.

No single authority assigns exact percentages to these domains.

However, converging evidence allows for **reasonable ranges** that reflect their relative impact on health and disease risk.

1. Mental & Emotional State / Belief System (≈40–50%)

Epigenetic research suggests that roughly 40–50% of variability in gene expression is shaped not by inherited DNA, but by environmental and psychosocial influences—including stress load, emotional patterns, mindset, and belief (Jirtle & Skinner, 2007).

Chronic psychological stress significantly increases the risk of cardiovascular disease, metabolic dysfunction, immune suppression, and mood disorders, accounting for a substantial portion of preventable illness (Cohen et al., 2007).

Psychoneuroimmunology demonstrates that emotional states can modulate immune activity by as much as 40–70%, shifting the body toward repair or degeneration depending on autonomic balance (Ader et al., 1995).

Even the placebo effect—the biological impact of expectation—accounts for a large proportion of outcomes in conditions such as pain, depression, and irritable bowel syndrome (Benedetti, 2014).

In short, the brain does not merely interpret reality—it chemically participates in shaping it.

Taken together, belief systems, stress perception, emotional regulation, and internal narrative exert influence over **nearly half of long-term health outcomes.**

2. Diet (≈20–25%)

Diet is the second most influential pillar.

The Global Burden of Disease Study estimates that dietary factors contribute to approximately 22% of adult deaths worldwide and account for roughly 20–25% of chronic disease burden (Afshin et al., 2019). Comparable figures appear in U.S. data linking poor nutrition to obesity, diabetes, cardiovascular disease, and systemic inflammation (CDC, 2022).

Food does far more than provide calories. It shapes the gut microbiome, regulates hormones, influences immune signaling, and alters inflammatory pathways.

Yet even optimal nutrition cannot override a chronically dysregulated nervous system. Many people "do everything right" nutritionally and still struggle—not because food failed, but because biology responds to belief first.

3. Sleep (≈15–20%)

Sleep is the foundation upon which all other health behaviors depend.

Research shows that even a single night of insufficient sleep alters the expression of hundreds of genes involved in inflammation, immune function, and cellular repair (Möller-Levet et al., 2013). Chronic sleep deprivation increases the risk of obesity, cardiovascular disease, depression, and all-cause mortality by approximately 15–25% (Cappuccio et al., 2010).

The National Institutes of Health estimates that sleep quality influences roughly 15–20% of long-term health outcomes (NIH, 2021).

Put simply, diet cannot compensate for chronic sleep loss, and exercise cannot undo its effects.

4. Exercise / Movement (≈10–15%)

Movement remains essential—but its isolated impact is often overstated.

Large cohort studies show that regular physical activity reduces mortality risk by approximately 10–20%, depending on intensity and consistency (Lear et al., 2017). Muscular strength predicts roughly 10–15% of long-term survival variance (Ruiz et al., 2008).

Exercise improves insulin sensitivity, cardiovascular health, mitochondrial function, hormone balance, and neuroplasticity. Its greatest power, however, lies in synergy: movement enhances sleep quality, amplifies dietary benefits, and stabilizes emotional regulation.

PULLING THE DATA TOGETHER

While these four domains are deeply interconnected, the evidence supports the following **approximate distribution** of influence on long-term health:

> **Mental & Emotional State / Belief System: 40–50%**
> **Diet: 20–25%**
> **Sleep: 15–20%**
> **Exercise / Movement: 10–15%**

This framework reinforces a central thesis of this book: **health begins on the inside.** When the internal environment is chaotic, no amount of external optimization can create lasting healing.

> Belief shapes biology.
> Mindset shapes metabolism.
> Emotion shapes immunity.
> Perception shapes physiology.

Modern science is now confirming what spiritual traditions have taught for millennia: healing starts within.

CHAPTER 7

THE PSYCHOLOGY OF SELF-HEALING

"Above all else, guard your heart, for
everything you do flows from it."
PROVERBS 4:23

HEALING BEGINS IN THE MIND

Healing is never only biological; it is deeply psychological. The way we think, feel, and interpret experience shapes hormones, immunity, and even gene expression. The nervous and endocrine systems respond faithfully to belief—often before conscious awareness catches up.

Every thought carries chemistry. Hope releases dopamine and oxytocin; fear releases cortisol and adrenaline. Over time, repeated emotional patterns become physiological instructions, confirming what the heart already believes to be true.

To understand the psychology of self-healing is to move from passive recipient to active participant—to recognize that recovery is not something done to us, but something awakened within us.

THE ROLE OF BELIEF AND SELF-EFFICACY

Psychologist Albert Bandura described self-efficacy as the belief in one's capacity to influence outcomes. High self-efficacy correlates not only with resilience and persistence, but with measurable biological advantages—lower stress hormones, stronger immune response, and faster recovery (Bandura, 1997).

Belief fuels behavior. Behavior rewires biology.

I see this principle daily in my fitness studio. Members who enter recovery practices with curiosity and confidence consistently progress faster than those burdened by doubt. Posture shifts. Breathing deepens. Endurance expands. The same stimulus produces different outcomes because expectation alters physiology.

Scripture names this dynamic plainly. After healing a woman long afflicted, Jesus said:

> *"Thy faith hath made thee whole."*
> **MARK 5:34, KJV**

Faith here is not wishful thinking—it is internal permission for the body to follow the mind's lead.

COGNITIVE RESTRUCTURING—
REWRITING INTERNAL NARRATIVES

Most limiting beliefs are inherited long before illness appears. Stories such as *this runs in my family, I'm fragile,* or *this is just aging* function as internal software, instructing the body to perform limitation.

Cognitive restructuring—a cornerstone of cognitive-behavioral therapy—identifies these scripts and replaces them with more accurate and empowering truths (Beck, 2011). One studio member living with chronic back pain shifted her self-concept from *my spine is weak* to *my body is resilient and learning safety again.* Within months, pain diminished and mobility improved—not by miracle, but by neuroplastic re-coding.

Research supports this shift. Cognitive reframing lowers cortisol, modulates inflammatory markers, and improves vagal tone (Davidson & McEwen, 2012). Neural networks once wired for vigilance begin reorganizing around recovery.

Paul anticipated this long before modern psychology:

> *"And be not conformed to this world: but be ye*
> *transformed by the renewing of your mind."*
> **ROMANS 12:2**

The renewal is literal—neural, hormonal, cellular.

HABIT FORMATION AND BEHAVIORAL ALIGNMENT

Belief must be embodied. Lasting change requires repetition—neural rehearsal that bridges intention and action.

Behavioral science shows that habits form through cue–routine–reward loops (Duhigg, 2012). In healing, these loops become sacred practices: mindful movement, breath-centered attention, and reflective journaling that reinforces progress.

At first, discipline leads. Over time, delight follows. Repetition sculpts the brain until health becomes automatic—the renewed mind made flesh.

EMOTIONAL COHERENCE AND THE BIOLOGY OF FEELING

If thought directs behavior, emotion powers it.

Unresolved grief, resentment, or shame keep the nervous system locked in defense. Physician Gabor Maté describes this stress–disease connection: chronic emotional suppression alters gene expression, increases inflammation, and accelerates aging (Maté, 2003).

Healing requires emotional literacy—awareness without judgment. Evidence-based practices include breathwork and meditation, which shift the body from vigilance to restoration; gratitude and loving-kindness, which activate growth-oriented neurochemistry; and community, which stabilizes immune function and reduces stress markers (Fredrickson et al., 2008; Cohen et al., 2012).

Emotion is energy in motion. When felt and released through awareness, it frees biology to repair.

INTEGRATING MINDSET, EMOTION, AND ACTION

Self-healing operates through a dynamic triad:

- **Mindset—Belief:** Identify limiting narratives; replace them with truth and possibility.

- **Behavior—Action:** Translate belief into embodied routines.

- **Emotion—Coherence:** Regulate the heart to stabilize the system.

These elements reinforce one another. Empowered belief drives action. Consistent action strengthens neural wiring. Emotional coherence sustains balance. The result is psychophysiological resilience—body and spirit functioning as unified intelligence.

In my own journey, this triad became lived theology. When pain lingered, I learned to ask not *what is broken?* but *what am I believing?*

Each shift—from frustration to gratitude, fear to faith—was followed by physiological change. Healing became discipleship: thought, emotion, and action aligning in worshipful coherence.

PRACTICAL PATHWAYS FOR PSYCHOLOGICAL HEALING

- **Renew the Narrative:** Speak affirmations grounded in truth—*my body is intelligent and responsive to peace.*

- **Practice Presence:** Use slow breathing or prayer to anchor awareness in the present moment.

- **Create Micro-Habits:** Attach new behaviors to existing routines.

- **Connect in Community:** Healing multiplies in shared intention.

- **Guard the Heart:** Filter inputs—media, relationships, and thoughts—through love and faith. What enters the heart programs the body.

CLOSING INSIGHT

The psychology of self-healing is not about willpower; it is about remembrance. The body remembers every thought, every emotion, every story we tell ourselves.

When we choose faith over fear and coherence over chaos, the nervous system rewrites its instructions.

Healing is less about fixing what is wrong and more about remembering what has always been right within us. Guard the heart wisely, guide it gently—and grace will flow through every cell.

CHAPTER 8

THE NEUROSCIENCE OF BELIEF

How Thoughts Shape Reality

*"For as he thinketh in his heart, so is he: Eat and drink,
saith he to thee; but his heart is not with thee."*

PROVERBS 23:7

BELIEF AS THE ARCHITECT OF EXPERIENCE

Every human being lives inside a story shaped by belief. Thoughts are not random; they function as instructions. Beliefs are not invisible; they organize perception, behavior, and physiology.

Modern neuroscience confirms what spiritual traditions have long asserted: the way we interpret reality strongly influences how we experience it—biologically and behaviorally.

For much of modern history, psychology treated thought as abstract and biology as concrete. That divide has collapsed. Thought and biology are not separate systems but interdependent processes. Every belief sends electrochemical signals through the nervous system, shaping hormones, immune response, and sensory interpretation.

In practical terms, we do not experience reality as it is—we experience reality as it is filtered through belief.

Ellen Langer's Counterclockwise study illustrated this vividly. Older adults immersed in an environment reflecting a younger identity showed measurable physiological improvement—posture, vision, strength, and cognition all improved. Belief altered biological expression (Langer, 2009).

THE BRAIN AS A PREDICTION ENGINE

Contemporary neuroscience describes the brain as a prediction system—constantly anticipating the next moment based on prior belief and experience. Perception is not passive observation; it is active construction.

The brain generates an internal model of reality and filters sensory input to match that model. When pain is expected, neural circuits amplify pain signals. When safety is expected, those same signals are dampened. Fear intensifies suffering; faith reduces its grip.

As Lynne Zimmerman explains, belief functions as a sensory directive—an internal reference point guiding how the nervous system interprets and responds to experience (Zimmerman, 2019).

Belief, then, is not a mental accessory. It is a governing process.

THE BIOLOGY OF BELIEF

Bruce Lipton demonstrated that perception influences genetic expression. The same gene can yield different outcomes depending on the internal signals it receives (Lipton, 2015).

Fear-based perception activates defensive chemistry—stress hormones and inflammatory pathways. Perceptions rooted in trust and safety activate growth-related signaling associated with repair and regeneration.

Lipton summarizes this insight simply:

> "When you change the way you see the world, you change the world you see."

Scripture describes a parallel process:

> *"And be not conformed to this world: but be ye transformed by the renewing of your mind."*
> ROMANS 12:2, KJV

The renewal Paul described aligns with what biology now observes: sustained changes in thought reshape internal signaling, which reshapes the body.

BELIEF, EMOTION, AND NEURAL REINFORCEMENT

David Hamilton's work in psychoneuroimmunology demonstrates how visualization and expectation influence wound healing, cardiovascular function, and immune response (Hamilton, 2018).

Neural circuits strengthen through repetition paired with emotion. Thought alone has limited impact; thought combined with feeling becomes instruction. When belief is consistently paired with gratitude or peace, neural networks reorganize toward coherence. When belief is paired with fear, the body complies just as faithfully.

Belief, emotion, and attention form a closed biological feedback loop. Sustained fear promotes illness. Sustained coherence supports recovery.

VIKTOR FRANKL
AND THE SPACE OF AGENCY

Viktor Frankl observed that individuals who retained meaning often survived conditions that should have been unsurvivable. He described a crucial space between stimulus and response—the moment where interpretation occurs.

Neuroscientifically, this is where the prefrontal cortex can override fear-based reactivity. Spiritually, it is the locus of agency. In that space, belief reshapes experience.

ATTENTION, AWARENESS,
AND POSSIBILITY

Joe Dispenza extends these principles using the language of focused attention and possibility. While quantum metaphors must be applied carefully, the practical insight aligns with neuroscience: sustained attention reshapes neural circuits and bodily response.

Habitual focus becomes the environment the brain and body inhabit. Attention directed toward pain strengthens pain circuits. Attention directed toward peace or possibility strengthens adaptive regulation.

Jesus expressed this principle without scientific framing:

"According to your faith be it unto you."
MATTHEW 9:29

Belief directs perception. Perception shapes experience.

BELIEF, NEUROPLASTICITY,
AND THE CREATIVE BRAIN

Neuroplasticity makes belief a physical force. Repeated thought strengthens specific neural pathways until belief becomes automatic perception.

Daniel Siegel refers to this process as *mindsight*: awareness shaping the physical architecture of the brain. Practices such as meditation, prayer, and visualization create neural networks that support regulation, resilience, and coherence (Siegel, 2010).

What we consistently hold in mind, the body holds in form.

FAITH, FOCUS, AND RENEWED PERCEPTION

Faith is not denial of reality; it is disciplined focus. It chooses possibility where habit expects limitation.

Paul captured this orientation succinctly:

> *"For we walk by faith, not by sight."*
> 2 CORINTHIANS 5:7

Sight follows expectation—not the other way around. To change experience, focus must change. The brain—and the body—will follow.

PRACTICAL PATHWAYS— TRAINING BELIEF

- **Conscious Observation:** Notice expectations and redirect attention toward gratitude.

- **Visualization:** Rehearse desired outcomes with sensory detail.

- **Emotional Alignment:** Pair belief with calm or gratitude.

- **Faith Journaling:** Record evidence of progress to reinforce belief through experience.

- **Environment of Expectation:** Choose language, relationships, and imagery that affirm wholeness.

These practices transform belief from concept into biology—and biology into change.

CLOSING INSIGHT

The neuroscience of belief confirms what Scripture has long taught: inner orientation shapes lived reality. When belief is rooted in limitation, experience follows suit. When belief aligns with wholeness, the body responds accordingly.

Every thought leaves a trace. To heal, to grow, to create, belief must lead—and life will follow.

PART III

THE SPIRITUAL DIMENSION

CHAPTER 9

PRAYER, FAITH, AND HEALING

"Therefore I say unto you, What things soever ye desire, when ye pray, believe that ye receive them, and ye shall have them."

MARK 11:24

THE MEETING PLACE OF SCIENCE AND SPIRIT

Prayer has long been understood as the language of the soul—a private communion between humanity and the Divine. Modern neuroscience now describes prayer in measurable terms: as a physiological event that reshapes neural circuits, regulates hormones, and supports immune balance.

In this way, prayer bridges two realms: the unseen world of intention and the visible world of biology. Faith—the inner posture of expectancy—acts as the conductor between them. Together, prayer and faith form one of the oldest and most accessible healing practices known to humanity.

What Scripture names devotion, science now recognizes as coherence.

THE NEUROSCIENCE OF PRAYER

Research in neurotheology shows that sustained prayer and meditation increase activity in the prefrontal cortex—associated with focus, compassion, and regulation—while quieting the amygdala, the brain's primary fear center (Newberg, 2018).

This shift produces measurable physiological effects. Stress hormones decrease. Immune signaling improves. Vagal tone strengthens, enhancing communication between brain and body.

Scripture expresses this truth succinctly:

> *"Perfect love casts out fear."*
> 1 JOHN 4:18, KJV

When fear subsides, the body's intrinsic capacity for repair is no longer suppressed. Prayer, then, is not an escape from reality—it is regulation of it.

FAITH AS NEUROBIOLOGICAL ALIGNMENT

Faith is not passive optimism; it is biological orientation.

Belief in a positive outcome activates reward and regulation pathways in the brain, releasing neurochemicals associated with trust, bonding, and repair (Hamilton, 2018). This same mechanism underlies the placebo effect: expectation producing genuine physiological change.

From an epigenetic perspective, perception of safety or threat influences which genes are expressed. Fear signals activate defense. Faith signals support growth and restoration (Lipton, 2015).

Scripture names this alignment plainly:

"Thy faith hath made thee whole."
MARK 5:34

What Christ described relationally, neuroscience observes biologically: coherence between thought, emotion, and physiology.

PRAYER, PERCEPTION, AND CELLULAR RESPONSE

Research now extends this understanding to the level of gene expression. Studies show that meditation and prayerful contemplation can reduce inflammatory gene activity and influence metabolic and immune pathways within hours (Kaliman et al., 2014; Bhasin et al., 2013).

These practices engage many of the same biological pathways targeted by medication—without adverse effects. They shift the body from defense into repair.

Faith, then, is not passive belief but participatory alignment. Prayer sends a coherent signal through the nervous system declaring safety, order, and trust. Cells respond accordingly.

MY STORY: WHEN PRAYER BECAME PHYSIOLOGY

During recovery from service-related injuries, I prayed earnestly—but often without expectation. My words asked for healing while my beliefs quietly anticipated limitation. The body reflected that conflict. Progress stalled.

As I studied neuroscience alongside the Gospels, a realization emerged: prayer was less about asking and more about aligning. I stopped praying *for* healing and began praying *from* healing—offering gratitude as if restoration were already complete.

Within weeks, inflammation decreased, pain softened, and energy returned. Medical charts offered no clear explanation. Faith did. Prayer had moved from language to wiring.

PRAYER AS COGNITIVE AND EMOTIONAL TRAINING

From a psychological perspective, prayer functions as focused cognitive restructuring. It redirects attention from fear toward trust, gradually reshaping neural expectations.

Regular prayer strengthens communication between the prefrontal cortex and limbic system, improving emotional regulation and stress tolerance (Siegel, 2010). Scripture anticipated this relationally:

> *"Be careful for nothing; but in every thing by prayer and supplication with thanksgiving let your requests be made known unto God. And the peace of God… shall keep your hearts and minds through Christ Jesus."*
> **PHILIPPIANS 4:6–7**

Peace here is not abstract. It functions as protection—stabilizing thought, emotion, and bodily response. Prayer is not passive hope; it is active mental and emotional training.

PRAYER, COMMUNITY, AND COLLECTIVE COHERENCE

While personal prayer reshapes the individual, communal prayer amplifies coherence. Studies show that synchronized group intention reduces stress markers and increases emotional stability across participants.

Research describes this as social coherence—the alignment of multiple nervous systems in compassionate resonance (McCraty et al., 2009).

Scripture names the same reality:

> *"For where two or three are gathered together in*
> *my name, there am I in the midst of them."*
> MATTHEW 18:20

The presence is relational, but its effects are measurable—greater harmony than any individual alone.

MAKING PRAYER EMBODIED

Prayer becomes most powerful when it is embodied:

- **Shift from Petition to Alignment:** Pray from gratitude, as if restoration is already underway.

- **Pair Prayer with Breath:** Slow breathing synchronizes heart and brain.

- **Integrate Visualization:** Imagine wholeness vividly.

- **Pray Through the Body:** Combine prayer with stillness or gentle movement.

- **Practice Collective Intention:** Shared prayer strengthens coherence and accountability.

Each practice transforms prayer from abstraction into biological instruction—a rehearsal of divine order within the body.

CLOSING INSIGHT

Prayer and faith are not opposites of science; they reveal the science of Spirit. They restore consciousness as the missing variable in healing.

When thought, emotion, and physiology align in awareness of God, the body remembers its original design. Healing ceases to be something pursued and becomes something recalled.

Faith renders the unseen coherent, the intangible measurable, and the hoped-for real.

CHAPTER 10

GRATITUDE, JOY, AND FLOW STATES

"…for the joy of the Lord is your strength."
NEHEMIAH 8:10

THE ENERGY OF ELEVATED EMOTION

If faith initiates healing, emotion sustains it.

Gratitude, joy, and awe are not merely pleasant feelings; they are elevated emotional states that harmonize the nervous system, reduce inflammation, and increase physiological resilience. When practiced intentionally, these emotions draw the body into coherence—a measurable state in which heart, brain, and spirit operate in synchrony.

Gratitude and joy are not optional luxuries. They are biological medicines embedded in our design. They expand perception, synchronize internal rhythms, and create the conditions in which healing becomes not forced, but natural.

Psychologist Barbara Fredrickson describes this phenomenon as the broaden-and-build effect: positive emotions widen awareness and build lasting psychological and biological resources (Fredrickson, 2008).

Scripture names this reality simply: **the joy of the Lord is strength.**

GRATITUDE AS BIOLOGICAL RECALIBRATION

Gratitude functions as both a spiritual posture and a physiological reset.

Neuroscience shows that gratitude activates reward circuitry in the brain, increasing dopamine and serotonin while lowering cortisol. At the cardiovascular level, gratitude stabilizes heart-rate variability, signaling safety to the autonomic nervous system. Research demonstrates that sustained appreciation produces measurable coherence between heart and brain, balancing the entire system (McCraty et al., 2009).

David Hamilton refers to gratitude as *the emotional signature of healing*—a signal to the body that the environment is safe enough for growth, repair, and regeneration (Hamilton, 2018).

Scripture frames gratitude as an act of faith rather than reaction. When Jesus prayed before miracles, He did not wait for outcomes— He gave thanks in advance:

> *"Father, I thank thee that thou hast heard me."*
> JOHN 11:41, KJV

Gratitude is the physiology of trust.

JOY AS STRENGTH AND MEDICINE

Joy, like gratitude, is not dependent on circumstance but on perception.

"A merry heart doeth good like a medicine: but a broken spirit drieth the bones." (*Proverbs 17:22*)

This is not poetic exaggeration; it is biological truth. Joy releases endorphins, oxytocin, and nitric oxide—chemicals associated with pain reduction, vascular health, and tissue repair (Davidson & McEwen, 2012). Research shows that joyful individuals exhibit greater left-prefrontal cortex activation, a marker of emotional stability, empathy, and adaptive resilience.

Joy literally rewires the brain toward health.

Importantly, joy is not denial of pain. It is the decision to perceive divine order even within difficulty. Joy lifts the body out of defense and into engagement. It prepares the nervous system for flow.

FLOW: THE SCIENCE OF IMMERSION

When gratitude and joy become sustained states, they naturally evolve into what Mihály Csikszentmihályi called *flow*—a condition of effortless immersion in which self-consciousness fades and presence takes over (Csikszentmihályi, 1990).

In flow, brain chemistry shifts into harmony. Activity in regions associated with self-criticism and time awareness decreases, while neurotransmitters linked to focus and pleasure rise. Movement becomes intuitive. Attention sharpens. Effort gives way to ease.

Flow is the biological expression of surrender.

MY JOURNEY: LEARNING TO RELEASE THE BRAKES

I did not understand flow until life insisted I feel it.

At a line-dancing class, I focused so intensely on getting each step right that I missed the music entirely. Others closed their eyes, moving effortlessly, carried by rhythm rather than control. They were not thinking—they were being.

The lesson repeated itself on motorcycle rides through the winding roads of Skyline Drive. Experienced riders leaned naturally into curves, merging with the road's rhythm. I gripped the handlebars, tense and overcorrecting, braking where trust was required. They flowed; I fought.

And again while kayaking the Potomac River. Seasoned paddlers rolled with the current, recovering easily after capsizing. I resisted, bailed out, and clung to control.

Over time, the truth became undeniable: **flow requires faith**. Not belief in technique, but trust in the process. Gratitude opens the door to that trust. Joy sustains it.

Flow, at its core, is the nervous system's expression of belief.

THE THEOLOGY OF FLOW

Flow is not merely psychological; it is profoundly spiritual.

In Scripture, flow mirrors surrender to divine timing—movement aligned with purpose rather than forced by will. Jesus often spoke from this posture:

> *"My hour is not yet come."*
> **JOHN 2:4**

Mastery, in this sense, arises not from control, but from attunement. Paul describes the same reality:

> *"For in him we live, and move, and have our being."*
> **ACTS 17:28**

This is the language of flow—life lived within divine rhythm, sustained by something greater than effort alone.

When we stop overthinking every step, we enter the dance of faith. When we stop resisting every curve, we discover the path was already prepared. Flow is not the loss of control; it is the recognition that control was never ours to begin with.

THE NEUROTHEOLOGY OF JOY AND FLOW

Neuroimaging studies of flow show decreased activity in regions associated with self-criticism and time awareness—a state known as transient hypofrontality (Csikszentmihályi, 1990). Intuition, instinct, and Spirit lead.

Scripture names this paradox:

> *"For whosoever will save his life shall lose it: and*
> *whosoever will lose his life for my sake shall find it."*
> MATTHEW 16:25

To lose the self is to enter divine flow.

In this state, heart and brain synchronize. Gratitude becomes guidance. Joy becomes momentum. Prayer becomes motion.

TRAINING THE HEART FOR FLOW

- **Gratitude Journaling:** Begin and end each day naming three blessings. Feel them until the body softens.

- **Joyful Movement:** Dance, walk, or stretch without performance. Let movement express presence.

- **Release Control:** In moments of tension, breathe slowly and affirm trust.

- **Follow the Music:** In work, relationships, and creativity, trade control for rhythm.

- **Observe Nature:** Rivers, trees, and birds reveal how life flows when it remembers its source.

Flow begins where fear ends. Fear ends where faith begins.

CLOSING INSIGHT

Gratitude, joy, and flow are not separate virtues—they are stages of surrender.

Gratitude opens the heart.

Joy harmonizes the mind.

Flow unites them in divine rhythm.

Every cell, heartbeat, and breath moves to the music of faith when resistance fades. Healing is not forced; it is allowed.

The dancers, the riders, the paddlers—all discovered the same truth: life flows best when we trust the current.

"Be still, and know that I am God." (*Psalm 46:10*)

Stillness is not stagnation—it is rhythm remembered.

CHAPTER 11

BIBLICAL HERMENEUTICS AND HEALTH

*"And be not conformed to this world: but be ye transformed
by the renewing of your mind, that ye may prove what
is that good, and acceptable, and perfect, will of God."*
ROMANS 12:2

SCRIPTURE AS A LIVING TEXT OF WHOLENESS

For much of my life, I read the Bible as a collection of moral lessons and distant miracles—a sacred text to be admired rather than embodied. As I began studying neuroscience, epigenetics, and psychology, that understanding shifted. Scripture no longer appeared as spiritual poetry alone; it revealed itself as instruction for living—mentally, emotionally, and physically whole.

Biblical hermeneutics—the art of interpretation—asks how meaning unfolds as understanding deepens. When Scripture is read through a lens of integration rather than separation, it becomes a guide for coherence between thought and form, heaven and earth, mind and matter.

Genesis speaks to this coherence directly:

*"So God created man in his own image, in
the image of God created he him."*
GENESIS 1:27, KJV

That likeness is not limited to physical form. It includes consciousness itself. Just as God speaks creation into being, human beings participate in creation through word, attention, and belief. Scripture's
opening verses describe not only historical origins, but a living process still unfolding—thought becoming word, word becoming form.

THE LOST LANGUAGE OF EMBODIMENT

Over time, religion has often divided spirit from body, treating the
physical self as temporary or corruptible. Yet Scripture makes no such
separation. The body is called:

"The temple of the Holy Ghost."
1 CORINTHIANS 6:19

Not a cage for the soul, but its instrument—a living sanctuary
through which divine intelligence is expressed.

When this embodied understanding is lost, illness is interpreted
as punishment and healing as exception. But the biblical narrative
presents healing as restoration—a return to alignment with divine
order rather than a violation of natural law.

Scripture speaks this restoration plainly:

"Bless the Lord, O my soul… who healeth all thy diseases."
PSALM 103:2–3

To bless is to speak well—to align tongue, heart, and intention. Physiologically, this mirrors what science now describes as coherent emotional signaling. Modern research calls it self-directed neuroplasticity. The ancients called it prayer.

FAITH AS THE MECHANISM OF HEALING

Jesus never treated faith as superstition. He treated it as law.

Repeatedly, He said:

> *"Thy faith hath made thee whole."*
> **MARK 5:34**

In each case, belief—not circumstance—determined the outcome. Faith was the spiritual language for what neuroscience now recognizes as expectation-driven biology.

When the woman with the issue of blood touched Christ's garment, healing was not imposed from without; it was activated from within. Her body responded to an instruction already written by belief.

I encountered this truth personally. After retiring from the Army, I accepted my diagnoses as identity. Medical records became my gospel of limitation. When I began reading Scripture through the lens of belief shaping biology, something changed. As identity shifted from broken to whole, healing followed.

Faith became my therapy. Scripture became my neural code.

THE HERMENEUTICS OF HEALING MIRACLES

Every healing miracle in the Bible carries both physical and metaphysical meaning.

When Jesus said:

> *"Rise, take up thy bed, and walk."*
> **JOHN 5:8**

He addressed more than muscle. The bed represented the story of limitation the man had been lying in. Rising symbolized consciousness transcending its conditioning.

Restoring sight was never only about vision—it was about perception. These acts were not suspensions of natural law, but demonstrations of its deeper order.

What Jesus revealed spiritually, modern research now describes biologically. Belief alters cellular communication; expectation modulates healing chemistry. The Gospels and neuroscience speak the same truth in different dialects.

THE RENEWAL OF MIND AND MATTER

Romans 12:2 is not metaphorical language; it is instructional:

> *"And be not conformed to this world: but be ye*
> *transformed by the renewing of your mind."*
> **ROMANS 12:2**

The Greek *metamorphoō* means to change form. Paul was not describing moral polish, but transformation at the level of being.

Modern research confirms this insight. Ellen Langer's *Counterclockwise* study demonstrated that environments reinforcing youthful identity produced measurable biological rejuvenation. Bodies followed belief.

Transformation begins in perception and culminates in physiology.

ANCIENT WITNESSES TO THE SAME LAW

My encounter with Buddhist thought did not begin as a theological exploration, but as a relational one. Years ago, I learned that my brother and his wife—who is from Thailand—were practicing Buddhism. Out of respect and curiosity, I listened more carefully. What surprised me was not doctrinal agreement, but functional familiarity. The language was different. The conclusions were not theological. Yet the observations about the mind felt strangely recognizable.

At the time, I was already wrestling with questions of suffering, identity, and healing—both personally and professionally. I was not searching for a new belief system; I was searching for understanding. What I found instead was resonance at the level of mechanism. Buddhism approached suffering through disciplined inner observation rather than divine relationship, yet many of its insights into mind and embodiment mirrored principles I was encountering in Scripture and neuroscience alike.

One of Buddhism's oldest texts, the *Dhammapada*, states:

> *"Mind precedes all mental states. Mind is*
> *their chief; they are all mind-made."*
> **DHAMMAPADA 1–2**

I did not read this as contradiction, but as echo. Where Scripture speaks of the heart as the wellspring of life (Proverbs 4:23), Buddhism speaks of the mind as the forerunner of experience. Different terms—same discovery. Inner orientation shapes outer reality.

As my own healing journey deepened, this convergence became harder to ignore. Central to Buddhist practice is *Right View*—the discipline of perceiving reality accurately rather than through fear, conditioning, or false identity. Healing, in this framework, begins not by changing circumstances, but by correcting perception.

Paul describes the same process relationally when he urges believers:

> *"And be not conformed to this world: but be ye transformed by the renewing of your mind."*
> **ROMANS 12:2**

Here, transformation is not moral polish; it is perceptual realignment. The language is theological, but the mechanism is the same.

Another core Buddhist principle, *Dependent Origination*, teaches that nothing arises in isolation. Change the conditions, and the outcome changes. Scripture names this same law relationally:

> *"Be not deceived; God is not mocked: for whatsoever a man soweth, that shall he also reap."*
> **GALATIANS 6:7**

Hermetic philosophy calls this Cause and Effect. Biology now calls it epigenetics. The vocabulary differs; the process does not.

Even Buddhist mindfulness—often misunderstood as passive awareness—began to look familiar as my own practices of prayer and stillness deepened. Scripture instructs:

> *"Be still, and know that I am God."*
> **PSALM 46:10**

Both traditions point toward the same physiological shift modern science associates with parasympathetic regulation and neural coherence. Stillness is not disengagement from God; it is the quieting of interference so truth can be perceived.

What struck me most was this: Buddhism does not teach that a person *is* their suffering. It teaches that suffering intensifies when identity fuses with sensation or story. This aligns precisely with the Gospel pattern of healing. Jesus never reinforced illness identity. He consistently called people out of the narratives they were lying in—"Rise," "See," "Go"—each command restoring agency before restoring function.

Seen this way, Buddhist insight did not threaten my faith; it clarified a law Scripture reveals most fully. Across traditions, cultures, and centuries, one truth remained consistent: life follows belief. When the inner world is brought into alignment, the outer world follows.

For me, these encounters were not abstract comparisons. They arrived at specific moments, answering questions I was already living. Each became another confirmation—not that all paths are the same, but that truth leaves fingerprints everywhere. Scripture gave meaning. Science gave measurement. These ancient witnesses gave perspective. Together, they pointed to the same conclusion: healing begins within, and coherence is the language the body understands.

THE BIBLE AS EMBODIED INSTRUCTION

When I began reading the Bible not as distant history but as internal anatomy, the text came alive.

> "Keep thy heart with all diligence." (*Proverbs 4:23*)—
> heart–brain coherence.

> "Be still, and know that I am God." (*Psalm 46:10*)—
> parasympathetic regulation.

> "Let the weak say, I am strong." (*Joel 3:10*)—
> belief spoken into biology.

Scripture became less about memorization and more about incarnation.

PRACTICAL HERMENEUTICS FOR HEALING

- **Read Through the Body:** Don't only analyze—feel.

- **Translate Word into Action:** When Scripture says *rise*, stand.

- **Anchor Promises in Gratitude:** Give thanks as if fulfillment is already unfolding.

- **Release Fear-Based Interpretation:** Ask not *what am I doing wrong?* but *what am I being invited to remember?*

- **Live the Text:** Scripture is fulfilled when embodied.

CLOSING INSIGHT

When read through the lens of wholeness, the Bible ceases to be a book of rules and becomes a book of resonance—a guide for remembering who we already are.

Faith, prayer, gratitude, and love are not merely religious acts; they are technologies of restoration. They renew the mind, reorganize the body, and realign us with the divine blueprint written into every cell.

The Gospel of health was never hidden—it was waiting to be re-read.

"As Christ said, behold, the kingdom of God is within you."
LUKE 17:21

Within that kingdom—mind, body, and spirit—lies every healing we will ever need.

PART IV

THE PRACTICE OF ALIGNMENT

CHAPTER 12

CREATING YOUR HEALTH ECOSYSTEM

*"By wisdom a house is built, and through
understanding it is established."*
PROVERBS 24:3–4

THE ENVIRONMENT AS
AN EXTENSION OF BELIEF

Every cell in your body listens to its environment. So does your mind. We often assume health begins with behavior—what we eat, how we move, how we rest—but behavior is shaped by something even more powerful: the ecosystem we live in.

Your health ecosystem includes everything that surrounds and influences your internal state—your home, workspace, relationships, spiritual community, and the unseen atmosphere of your thoughts. It is the soil in which beliefs grow or wither.

Bruce Lipton demonstrated that cells do not act independently; they respond to environmental signals. Place a cell in a nourishing medium and it thrives. Place it in a toxic one and it deteriorates—even when its DNA is identical (Lipton, 2015). Humans are no different.

We are living collectives of trillions of cells responding to the bio-chemical "medium" shaped by emotion, thought, and surroundings.

If belief shapes biology, environment shapes belief. The two form a feedback loop: the spaces we inhabit reinforce the stories we tell, and those stories shape the signals our bodies interpret as truth.

THE ECOLOGY OF ENERGY

When I left the military, I was accustomed to environments defined by control—rules, structure, precision. That approach can serve a mission, but it can sabotage recovery. My home, routines, and inner dialogue still carried command-and-control energy.

Healing required more than discipline. It required environment.

Creating a health ecosystem meant surrounding myself with cues of peace rather than stress. I began paying attention to light, order, sensory input, and the emotional tone of a room. In my fitness studio, I saw it daily: warmth, infrared energy, and clean design shifted physiology before anyone ever moved. The environment itself carried intention.

And I realized something else: transformation didn't begin when people started exercising. It began the moment they walked through the door. The atmosphere spoke before I ever said a word.

Our homes and minds work the same way. Our surroundings constantly preach sermons our bodies believe.

(And yes—your nervous system is listening even when you insist you're "fine.")

THE NEUROSCIENCE
OF PLACE AND HABIT

Environment strongly influences habit formation. Context cues—visual, auditory, and social—trigger predictable neural pathways

(Duhigg, 2012). If your living room is associated with television and snacking, your brain will cue that routine automatically. Change the cue, and you change the pattern.

James Clear emphasizes that small changes in environment can produce massive changes in identity-based behavior (Clear, 2018). Joe Dispenza extends this idea into consciousness: if you want to change your personal reality, you must change your state of being—and one of the fastest ways to shift state is to redesign the cues that keep you anchored to your old self (Dispenza, 2017).

Your surroundings are never neutral. They either reinforce your aligned identity—or rehearse your former one.

BUILDING A TEMPLE, NOT A GYM

Scripture often describes transformation through construction: "By wisdom a house is built." (*Proverbs 24:3, KJV*) The house symbolizes both body and life structure—an environment established through conscious design.

In my own journey, this became literal. Building a fitness studio wasn't only business; it was an act of alignment. I envisioned it as a modern temple of transformation—where heat, infrared energy, and belief met physiology. The workouts became rituals of discipline and release. The stillness after effort became its own kind of prayer.

Whether it's a home, an office, or a corner of a room, your space can function as sacred architecture—arranged with intention to cultivate peace, vitality, creativity, and rest. The ancient temple was not merely a meeting place; it was a resonant chamber. Your environment can serve the same purpose: shaping the conditions where your nervous system learns safety and your body remembers repair.

THE SPIRITUAL
ECOLOGY OF RELATIONSHIPS

No ecosystem thrives in isolation. The people you spend time with are part of your health environment, too.

Scripture names this plainly: "Bad company corrupts good character." (*1 Corinthians 15:33*) In modern physiological terms, toxic relationships dysregulate the nervous system.

Relational energy is biological. Stress spreads. Calm spreads. Negativity and gratitude spread. Emotional states are contagious, and the body responds accordingly.

Surrounding yourself with people anchored in faith, joy, and purpose reinforces your own regulation and alignment. Healthy relationships are not optional; they are sacred nutrients.

THE SPIRITUAL
DISCIPLINE OF DESIGN

Designing a supportive environment is a form of devotion.

Genesis opens with God bringing order out of chaos—light, form, rhythm. Creation begins with separation and culminates in rest. The same sequence applies to healing: we separate what drains us from what sustains us, and then we rest in what remains.

When you cleanse a space, you are not merely organizing objects—you are reducing cognitive and emotional load. When you choose music that lifts your spirit, you are setting tone. Every sensory input—light, sound, color, scent—communicates to the subconscious what kind of life you expect to live.

In this way, environment becomes prayer made visible.

A PRACTICAL FRAMEWORK FOR BUILDING YOUR HEALTH ECOSYSTEM

1. Physical Environment—Your Outer Temple

- Declutter spaces associated with stress or stagnation.

- Create dedicated zones for prayer, rest, and renewal.

- Use natural light, warmth, plants, and calming scent to evoke peace.

- Place visual reminders of wholeness—Scripture, affirmations, symbols of growth.

2. Social Environment—Your Circle of Resonance

- Invest in relationships that reinforce your highest self.

- Set boundaries with chronic negativity and gossip—distance is sometimes devotion.

- Join communities that practice coherence: faith, fitness, service, or healing.

3. Internal Environment—Your Inner Atmosphere

- Begin each day with intention and gratitude.

- Replace mental clutter with breathwork or prayerful silence.

- Watch your inner dialogue: is it speaking blessing or fear? Rewrite it consciously.

4. Rhythmic Environment—Your Ecosystem of Time

- Structure the day around renewal cycles: morning reflection, mid-day reset, evening release.

- Honor Sabbath rhythms—rest as sacred necessity.

- Protect sleep as the body's nightly realignment with Spirit.

MY PRACTICE OF ALIGNMENT IN ACTION

Alignment became tangible for me only when I stopped treating life like a battlefield and started treating it like an ecosystem. The military taught control; faith taught connection. Healing began when I stopped fighting my environment and started designing it.

At home, I created an all-season space for restoration—filled with natural light and living plants, free from electronics and distraction. With expansive windows and a massage chair, it became the place where I slow my breathing, release accumulated stress, and allow my nervous system to return to calm. My fitness studio became a physical metaphor for alignment: heat as purification, sweat as surrender, and stillness as peace.

Environment, I discovered, is not background. It is theology—where Spirit meets structure.

CLOSING INSIGHT

We are not merely shaped by environment—we co-create it. Every word, object, habit, and relationship becomes part of the field that shapes our biology and our belief.

To build a health ecosystem is to build a modern sanctuary—where faith, intention, and daily rhythm support the body's design. Proverbs 24:3–4 offers the blueprint: wisdom designs the house, understanding establishes it, and knowledge fills it with good things.

Health is not something we chase. It is something we cultivate.

We don't have to escape the world to find peace. We simply have to build a world that believes with us.

CHAPTER 13

THE DAILY ALIGNMENT FORMULA

"They are new every morning: great is thy faithfulness."
LAMENTATIONS 3:23

LIVING IN RHYTHMS OF RENEWAL

Healing rarely arrives in dramatic moments. More often, it unfolds quietly—through rhythm. Just as the earth renews itself through sunrise and sunset, the body restores itself through repetition and rest. Health is not an event; it is a relationship lived daily between thought, body, and spirit.

The Daily Alignment Formula is not another routine to master or perfect. It is a way of living in harmony with divine design—aligning consciousness, physiology, and spirit so completely that healing becomes the natural byproduct of being.

In the Army, routine was survival. Discipline created readiness. At the time, that structure felt rigid, but later I recognized its deeper wisdom: what you do consistently matters far more than what you do occasionally. In the spiritual life, rhythm becomes sacred. Repetition becomes worship. Alignment becomes automatic.

THE SCIENCE
OF DAILY PRACTICE

Neuroscience confirms what spiritual tradition has always known: consistency—not intensity—drives transformation. Habits form through repetition; each thought or action strengthens the neural pathways associated with it (Doidge, 2007; Duhigg, 2012).

Joe Dispenza explains that every time we practice gratitude, presence, or visualization with intention, we fire and wire new neural circuits (Dispenza, 2017). Over time, intention becomes instinct. Bruce Lipton reminds us that perception and emotion send biochemical signals to every cell. Even a single consciously lived day can influence gene expression (Lipton, 2015).

The body learns through pattern. The mind learns through structure. The spirit moves through both.

MORNING—
SETTING THE FREQUENCY

Morning is sacred. It is the moment consciousness resets. How you begin the day determines the frequency your body carries forward.

During my doctoral studies, I began refining what I now call the **morning alignment triad**—three practices that synchronize belief, biology, and awareness before the noise of the world arrives.

1. Stillness and Breath

Before reaching for a phone—or even a thought—begin with presence. Sit or stand in stillness. Inhale slowly through the nose for four counts, hold for four, and exhale for six. This rhythm activates the parasympathetic nervous system, lowers stress hormones, and promotes heart–brain coherence (McCraty et al., 2009).

2. Gratitude and Declaration

Next, speak life. Name three things you are grateful for—specific, sensory, embodied. Then declare truth aloud:

- *My body is strong and wise.*

- *I am in harmony with divine health.*

- *Every cell in me is aligned with peace.*

Words create resonance. As Scripture reminds us:

> *"Death and life are in the power of the tongue."*
> **PROVERBS 18:21, KJV**

3. Movement and Energy Activation

Finally, move your body with intention rather than compulsion. Stretch, walk, or exercise mindfully.

I see this principle daily in my fitness studio: when members enter movement with clear intention—*I am healing, I am expanding*—endurance, performance, and recovery improve. The body follows the mind's lead.

MIDDAY—RESETTING COHERENCE

By midday, internal and external noise accumulates. Without interruption, the nervous system drifts toward reactivity. Alignment requires conscious recalibration.

1. The Three-Minute Reset

Pause. Close your eyes. Breathe in through the nose and out through the mouth. On each exhale, silently repeat the word *Release*.

This brief interruption shifts the nervous system toward balance and can reduce cortisol within minutes (Davidson & McEwen, 2012).

2. Nourishment with Awareness

Whether eating or hydrating, treat nourishment as communion. Bless your food. Chew slowly. Visualize it fueling vitality.

Gratitude alters digestive chemistry, improves nutrient absorption, and enhances metabolic efficiency (Hamilton, 2018). How you eat matters as much as what you eat.

3. Realignment Through Light or Movement

Step outside, even briefly. Natural light synchronizes circadian rhythms and supports hormonal balance by regulating cortisol and melatonin (Czeisler, 2013).

Creation provides its own reset button.

Alignment is not achieved once; it is remembered repeatedly.

EVENING—RECALIBRATION AND RESTORATION

Evening completes the cycle. Morning sets the tone; evening determines integration. Sleep is the body's daily resurrection—when hormones rebalance, memories consolidate, and cellular repair accelerates.

The goal of evening practice is not productivity, but release.

1. Reflection and Release

Before sleep, reflect briefly on three questions:

- What felt aligned today?

- What felt resistant or fearful?

- What can I bless and release?

This practice trains the brain to close the day in resolution rather than rumination (Siegel, 2010).

2. Gentle Movement or Breathwork

Engage in slow stretching or rhythmic breathing. Lengthen the exhale. Let the body soften.

This is not exercise—it is exhaling.

3. Scriptural or Spiritual Grounding

End the day with something sacred. Read a verse, speak gratitude, or visualize divine light moving gently through the body.

Psalm 4:8 remains a faithful companion:

> *"In peace I will both lay me down, and sleep: for*
> *thou, Lord, only makest me dwell in safety."*
>
> **PSALM 4:8**

When mind and spirit rest, the body follows.

THE 24-HOUR ALIGNMENT CYCLE

Time	Practice	Focus	Effect
Morning	Stillness, Gratitude, Movement	Activation	Sets frequency and intention
Midday	Breath, Light, Nourishment	Regulation	Restores coherence and energy
Evening	Reflection, Release, Grounding	Integration	Repairs body and mind through rest

Live one aligned day and you feel centered.

Live thirty and healing begins.

Live aligned for a year and identity itself transforms.

SPIRITUAL PARALLELS OF DAILY DISCIPLINE

Every major faith tradition honors rhythm as sacred technology. The Jewish Shema is recited morning and night. Monastic Christians structured prayer around canonical hours. Islam practices Salat five times daily, synchronizing movement, breath, and intention.

Discipline is devotion in motion. It is not legalism—it is design. When life becomes rhythm rather than reaction, health follows naturally.

PERSONAL REFLECTION— RHYTHM AS REVELATION

As I practiced these rhythms, pain softened, energy stabilized, and stress patterns quieted. I was not healed overnight—but I was no longer chaotic. Life began to feel musical again: structured, harmonious, and spacious between the notes.

Alignment is not achieved once; it is practiced daily. Each morning is a resurrection. Each night, a surrender. Each breath, a prayer.

CLOSING INSIGHT

Healing is not found in information; it is found in integration. The Daily Alignment Formula moves truth from the page into the body— where Scripture, science, and Spirit speak the same language:

Live consciously.

Move with gratitude.

Rest in peace.

Repeat.

When you live in rhythm with divine intelligence, your life becomes a liturgy of healing—a song your cells can hear.

CHAPTER 14

THE ALIGNMENT OF MIND, BODY, AND SPIRIT

Advanced Practices

"The mind governed by the Spirit is life and peace."
ROMANS 8:6

BEYOND BALANCE:
THE STATE OF COHERENCE

Alignment is not about balancing competing forces; it is about uniting them. In true coherence, mind, body, and spirit no longer operate as separate systems—they function as one integrated intelligence.

This is the next stage of healing. Once supportive environments and daily rhythms are established, we are invited into embodied awareness—a state in which spiritual truth and biological function merge seamlessly.

Research in neurotheology shows that sustained prayer and meditation reshape the brain. Activity increases in regions associated with regulation and compassion, while fear-based reactivity quiets (Newberg, 2018). Spirit, quite literally, rewires the nervous system.

In biblical language, this is renewal of the mind resulting in life and peace.

1. Breathwork—The Bridge Between Worlds

Breath is the most immediate and accessible pathway to alignment. From Scripture's opening pages, breath is presented as the interface between heaven and earth:

> *"And the Lord God formed man of the dust of the*
> *ground, and breathed into his nostrils the breath*
> *of life; and man became a living soul."*
> GENESIS 2:7, KJV

Breath stands between the involuntary and the intentional, the physical and the spiritual. Each breath carries instruction—safety or threat, peace or panic. Slow, diaphragmatic breathing stimulates the vagus nerve, activates parasympathetic calm, and synchronizes heart–brain coherence (McCraty et al., 2009).

In advanced practice, breath becomes prayer in motion:

- **Inhale (4 counts):** *Spirit within me.*

- **Hold (2 counts):** *I receive.*

- **Exhale (6 counts):** *Peace through me.*

Five minutes of conscious breathing can recalibrate physiology more effectively than an hour of willpower. When you guide the breath, you shape consciousness; when you release it, you practice trust.

2. Fasting—The Art of Spiritual Reset

Fasting is often misunderstood as deprivation, but Scripture presents it as preparation. Moses, Jesus, and Daniel fasted before moments of clarity and transformation.

Modern research confirms the biological wisdom behind the

practice. Short-term fasting activates autophagy—the body's cellular repair system—clearing damaged cells and resetting metabolic signaling (Longo & Panda, 2016).

I began fasting not to lose weight, but to listen more clearly. Hunger revealed emotional attachments as much as physical habits. As those loosened, awareness sharpened. Fasting reminded my body where provision truly comes from.

3. Visualization—Faith Rehearsed

Visualization is faith practiced internally before it appears externally. When imagined outcomes are paired with elevated emotion, the brain activates many of the same neural networks involved in physical action (Dispenza, 2017).

Scripture names this dynamic clearly:

> *"Now faith is the substance of things hoped*
> *for, the evidence of things not seen."*
> **HEBREWS 11:1**

Faith has substance because the nervous system treats what is believed as real. The body responds to meaning, expectation, and coherence—not merely to circumstance.

MY TEST OF BELIEF

Six months after shoulder surgery, pain returned—sharp, constant, and relentless. Imaging showed no tear, only arthritis and calcification. The diagnosis was final: chronic and irreversible.

This was no longer a medical challenge. It was a belief challenge.

Each evening, I visualized my shoulder fluid, mobile, and strong. I paired imagery with gratitude and Scripture:

"I will praise thee; for I am fearfully and wonderfully made."
PSALM 139:14

"But if the Spirit of him that raised up Jesus from the dead dwell in you… he shall also quicken your mortal bodies." (*Romans 8:11*)

There were nights when doubt was louder than faith. But belief, like muscle, strengthens under resistance. I continued—not perfectly, but consistently.

Over time, the pain subsided. Today, it is gone.

That experience healed more than my shoulder. It refined my faith. Every symptom became an invitation—not to fear—but to deeper alignment.

4. Silence—The Forgotten Medicine

We live in a culture saturated with noise. Yet Scripture calls us back to stillness:

"Be still, and know that I am God."
PSALM 46:10

Neuroscience shows that silence activates the brain's default mode network, enhancing emotional regulation, creativity, and self-awareness (Kühn et al., 2014). Silence restores what overstimulation fragments.

After years in the Army, stillness initially felt unsafe. Over time, I discovered silence was not absence—it was presence. Healing spoke quietly, but persistently.

5. Service—The Circulation of Spirit

Alignment completes itself through service. Healing that does not flow outward stagnates.

Research shows that compassion and contribution elevate oxytocin, serotonin, and immune function (Post, 2005). Kindness is contagious biology.

Scripture names this circulation:

> *"Give, and it shall be given unto you…*
> *running over."*
> LUKE 6:38

In my studios, I see this daily. Members who shift from self-focus to encouragement often experience the greatest transformation. Service turns discipline into devotion.

6. Integration—Living from the Inside Out

Advanced alignment is not about adding techniques; it is about becoming the practice. Breath becomes prayer. Body becomes temple. Life becomes liturgy.

When the inner world resonates with peace, the outer world reorganizes to match. This is not philosophy—it is physiology. Thought releases chemistry. Emotion shapes signaling. Coherence restores function.

ADVANCED ALIGNMENT PRACTICES

Practice	Focus	Scientific Effect	Spiritual Parallels
Breathwork	Nervous system balance	Increases HRV, reduces cortisol	"The breath of life" (Genesis 2:7)
Fasting	Metabolic & cellular reset	Activates autophagy; improves clarity	"Man shall not live by bread alone" (Matthew 4:4)
Visualization	Neural programming	Strengthens new circuits, accelerates healing	"Faith is the substance…" (Hebrews 11:1)

Practice	Focus	Scientific Effect	Spiritual Parallels
Silence	Mental restoration	Activates DMN, improves creativity	"Be still and know..." (Psalm 46:10)
Service	Emotional coherence	Boosts oxytocin, immunity, and empathy	"Give, and it will be given..." (Luke 6:38)

Together, these practices form a living loop: inward alignment, biological renewal, and outward circulation.

CLOSING INSIGHT

When mind, body, and spirit align, healing is no longer intervention—it is integration. Prayer becomes breath. Stillness becomes knowing. Service becomes joy.

You stop chasing miracles and begin living as one.

This is the Kingdom within—the state of coherence where Spirit directs biology and belief sustains being.

You were never meant to fight for health.

You were designed to flow in it.

PART V

THE PRACTICE OF BELIEVING

CHAPTER 15

BECOMING YOUR OWN HEALER

"The kingdom of God is within you."
LUKE 17:21

THE SHIFT FROM PATIENT TO PARTICIPANT

Healing begins when we stop waiting for someone else to save us. For much of modern history, medicine has trained people to become passive recipients—to look outward for prescriptions, procedures, and professionals who "fix" what feels broken. Yet Scripture and science point to a deeper truth: the body carries a God-given intelligence designed to heal, regenerate, and restore.

Each cell responds to its environment—to the chemical and emotional signals shaped by thought, belief, and expectation. The same mechanisms that translate fear into illness can translate faith into repair. When Jesus said, *"The kingdom of God is within you,"* He was not offering metaphor alone. He was naming reality: the power to renew is not only external; it is internal.

You are not broken.

You are not deficient.

You do not have to chase healing—you have to awaken to it.

THE INTERNAL PHYSICIAN

Your body already knows how to repair itself. Bones knit. Skin closes. The immune system adapts and remembers. This is not random biology; it is ordered intelligence embedded in creation.

Coherent states—gratitude, calm focus, elevated emotion—prepare the nervous system for repair. The body moves toward the future the mind rehearses. Healing, then, is often less about intervention and more about communication.

When mind, body, and spirit begin speaking the same language—the language of peace, faith, and expectation—the body follows that instruction.

A TEST OF INTEGRITY

After retiring from the Army, I promised myself I wouldn't become *that guy*—the one who slowly fades into stress, fatigue, and resignation. I had seen it too often: the sharp soldier becoming the tired veteran.

But life presses in. Metabolism shifts. Energy changes. The mirror begins reflecting someone you don't fully recognize.

Around that time, friends were turning to what looked like an easy solution—the weight-loss injection. I went through the process: the appointments, the paperwork, the plan. My goal was simple—get the prescription.

And then something in me stopped.

Here I was teaching belief, alignment, and coherence—yet preparing to outsource my own transformation. The question wasn't about judgment. It was about integrity. If I believed what I was writing, I had to live it—especially when it was inconvenient.

So I stopped.

I chose the slower path: the discipline of belief. Each morning, I stood before the mirror and faced the evidence of where I was. That reflection became a daily decision point. Would I believe what I saw—or what I knew to be true?

It wasn't easy. But something shifted. Workouts became declarations, not punishments. Gratitude became fuel. I began seeing myself healthy and strong before my body could confirm it.

And slowly—steadily—it did.

That season taught me what becoming your own healer actually means. Healing is not control. It is coherence. It is not denying evidence—it is giving the body a higher instruction and then living in a way that makes that instruction believable.

SCRIPTURE AND INNER AUTHORITY

In Scripture, healing is rarely passive. Jesus consistently invited participation:

"Wilt thou be made whole?"
JOHN 5:6, KJV

"Thy faith hath made thee whole."
MARK 5:34

Healing required belief, movement, and awareness. What was restored was not only tissue or function, but authority—the reclaiming of one's inner kingdom.

Scripture frames this responsibility clearly:

"Keep thy heart with all diligence;
for out of it are the issues of life."
PROVERBS 4:23

The heart here is the integrated center of belief, intention, perception, and direction. To guard it is not selfish—it is stewardship.

To believe in your own healing is not arrogance. It is agreement with divine intention.

WHAT SCIENCE CONFIRMS

Across neuroscience, epigenetics, and psychoneuroimmunology, one truth remains consistent: belief changes biology.

Expectation alters immune response.

Emotional states influence gene expression.

Coherent emotions synchronize heart, brain, and nervous system.

Your most repeated thoughts and sustained emotions become molecular instruction. Faith is not abstract—it is physiological.

BECOMING YOUR OWN HEALER— A LIVING FRAMEWORK

- **Observe the evidence without attachment.** Facts describe the present; belief shapes the trajectory.

- **Rewrite the inner script.** Speak life until it becomes familiar.

- **Create an environment of coherence.** Surround yourself with cues of peace, light, and support.

- **Feel it first.** Emotion bridges belief and physiology.

- **Trust the process.** Transformation unfolds steadily, not instantly.

THE MIRROR AND THE MESSAGE

Each morning, I faced the same choice: judge the reflection—or honor it.

I learned something simple and sobering: the body does not respond well to contempt. It responds to compassion.

Healing began when I stopped fighting the man in the mirror and started partnering with him. I realized I wasn't waiting for healing to happen—I was waiting to believe it already had.

Today, I see not perfection, but partnership—between mind and matter, between human effort and divine life. I became my own healer not by replacing God, but by aligning with Him.

CLOSING INSIGHT

Becoming your own healer means remembering that the power that made you is the power that sustains you.

You are not a broken machine waiting for repair.

You are a living design in constant renewal.

When you see yourself that way, healing stops being something you chase and becomes something you embody. Every breath, every belief, every act of gratitude becomes medicine.

You are both the patient and the practitioner.

The evidence—and the answer.

CHAPTER 16

SUSTAINING ALIGNMENT

Overcoming Setbacks and Staying On The Path

"And let us not be weary in well doing: for in due season we shall reap, if we faint not."
GALATIANS 6:9

THE REAL WORK BEGINS AFTER THE BREAKTHROUGH

Healing is rarely a single moment of revelation. More often, it is a rhythm.

The first experience of transformation—whether physical, emotional, or spiritual—can feel miraculous. Sustaining that alignment through daily life, doubt, criticism, and ordinary stress is where faith matures.

After every breakthrough, old patterns test the foundation. Familiar thoughts whisper, *Nothing really changed.* The body remembers pain. The world reflects old identities. True healing, then, is not defined by what happens once, but by what you continue to believe when visible evidence wavers.

RESILIENCE AND THE BIOLOGY OF RETURN

Resilience is not resistance; it is recovery.

Neuroscience defines resilience as a flexible nervous system—one that adapts to stress and returns to equilibrium rather than remaining trapped in survival mode (Davidson & McEwen, 2012). Stress responses are not failures; they are reflexes. What matters is how quickly the system remembers safety.

With repeated alignment practices—breath, prayer, stillness, gratitude—the brain learns that calm is safe rather than threatening. Research shows that consistent emotional regulation increases activity in regions associated with recovery and optimism. Simply put, bodies that expect repair tend to recover more efficiently.

Resilience is faith expressed through physiology.

GUARDING THE VISION AGAINST "EVIDENCE"

One of the most difficult aspects of sustaining alignment is not internal discomfort—it is external reinforcement of old identity.

During my recovery, comments from others—often casual, sometimes well-intentioned—reflected who I had been rather than who I was becoming. Remarks about pain, posture, or appearance became forms of *evidence*, anchoring attention to the past.

This is one of the great challenges of healing: the people we love can unknowingly reinforce the story we are outgrowing.

At times, those words lodged themselves in my mind. The temptation was subtle but powerful—to agree with appearances. Yet I had learned this truth before: evidence describes the present; belief shapes the direction.

So I stopped arguing with appearances and aligned more deeply with truth. When doubt surfaced, I returned to breath, stillness, and declaration—anchoring myself in the understanding that renewal is ongoing, not instant, and that the same Spirit who gives life dwells within us (*2 Corinthians 4:16; Romans 8:11*).

Over time, the comments lost their weight. Eventually, they became confirmation of how much discipline it takes to hold faith steady when the visible world lags behind internal change.

Sustaining alignment is not about silencing the outside world.

It is about establishing sovereignty within.

THE SCIENCE OF SETBACKS

Setbacks are not failures; they are recalibration points.

Healing does not occur in a straight line. The nervous system naturally oscillates between balance and imbalance as it rewires—a process known as allostasis, or stability through change (McEwen & Wingfield, 2010).

Fatigue, doubt, or the return of old sensations do not mean alignment is lost. Often, they signal deeper integration. Ellen Langer's research demonstrates that when belief and environment remain aligned, physiology follows. When attention drifts back to old identity cues, biology responds accordingly (Langer, 2009).

Setbacks occur when we forget who we are. Recovery begins the moment we remember.

WHEN FAITH FEELS FRAGILE

The greatest threat to sustained healing is not pain—it is doubt disguised as logic.

When progress slows, the mind demands proof. When proof feels absent, old programs reactivate: fear, comparison, impatience. This is not weakness; it is conditioning.

Relapse does not signal failure. It signals attention drift.

The work is not to eliminate relapse, but to shorten the return time. Each return strengthens the pathway. Each recovery reinforces trust.

Paul captured this dynamic simply:

"For we walk by faith, not by sight."
2 CORINTHIANS 5:7

Walking implies movement. Even unsteady steps still move forward.

SPIRITUAL ENDURANCE—
THE LONG VIEW

Every healing journey includes a wilderness season—the space between promise and manifestation. Even Christ faced temptation after clarity: the urge to prove what was already true.

Spiritual endurance is trusting divine timing. As Scripture reminds us, the harvest comes in due season—not immediately, but faithfully, if we do not abandon the path.

When belief becomes rhythm, faith becomes biology.

THE THREE-STEP
RETURN RITUAL

When alignment wavers—and it will—use this simple loop to return gently and effectively:

1. **Pause and Perceive:** Notice the trigger without judgment: fatigue, pain, criticism, or emotional drift.

2. **Breathe and Bless:** Use breath to restore coherence. Speak a truth aloud: *Peace governs my body. I am aligned with healing.*

3. **Reimagine and Release:** Visualize yourself restored. Release urgency. Return to flow.

Each return weakens the setback and strengthens the pathway. Mastery is not never leaving alignment—it is remembering how to return.

EMOTIONAL IMMUNITY— GUARDING THE HEART

Just as the immune system protects the body, emotional immunity protects alignment.

Chronic exposure to criticism, fear, or self-doubt weakens regulation over time. Emotional immunity is built through gratitude, forgiveness, and self-compassion.

Research shows that positive emotions expand cognitive flexibility and improve physiological health (Fredrickson et al., 2008). Love stabilizes what fear fragments.

Scripture names this plainly:

> *"Keep thy heart with all diligence;*
> *for out of it are the issues of life."*
> **PROVERBS 4:23**

This is not metaphor—it is instruction.

FAITH IN THE FACE OF EVIDENCE

Evidence speaks through test results, mirrors, memories, and the voices of others. Early on, I absorbed every message about limitation. They became mental graffiti.

But each time I noticed those messages settling in, I remembered: agreement shapes embodiment. What we accept internally, the body expresses externally.

So I learned to guard my inner dialogue deliberately. I didn't fight the words—I denied them residence.

Over time, defensiveness dissolved. Eventually, the same people who once emphasized my struggles began asking what had changed.

The answer was simple: I stopped listening to evidence and started listening to alignment.

CLOSING INSIGHT

Sustaining alignment is one of the highest expressions of faith.

It is not perfection, but persistence.

Not the absence of falls, but the certainty of return.

Each time you choose truth over appearance, gratitude over grievance, faith over fear, your biology listens. The nervous system settles. The body reorganizes. Healing becomes self-sustaining—not because challenges disappear, but because you have learned how to stand steady within them.

That is not merely health.

That is mastery.

YOUR PATH TO LIFELONG HEALTH

Integrating Mind, Body, And Spirit

"Even so faith, if it hath not works, is dead, being alone."
JAMES 2:17

THE MIRROR OF BELIEF

After decades of study, service, and personal trial, I have come to one unshakable conclusion: our lives, our bodies, and our health reflect what we believe to be true.

I meet people every day—faithful, sincere, prayerful people—who believe deeply in God's power yet live constrained by pain, fatigue, or quiet resignation. They pray for healing while speaking the language of defeat. They affirm faith while rehearsing fear. They profess divine wholeness while accepting chronic struggle as normal.

Their faith is not weak. It is simply unembodied.

Belief that never reaches the body remains incomplete. Healing requires agreement—mind, emotion, and physiology speaking the same message:

I am already whole.

When that agreement is established, faith stops being theory and becomes physiology.

FAITH, PHYSIOLOGY, AND THE TYRANNY OF EVIDENCE

We have been trained to trust evidence above all else—the doctor's report, the diagnosis, the mirror, the scale, the genetic test. These markers feel authoritative, but they are only snapshots of a system in constant change.

Modern science calls this epigenetic expression: the body continually rewrites itself in response to thought, emotion, and environment (Lipton, 2015). Scripture said it long before laboratories could measure it:

"For as he thinketh in his heart, so is he."
PROVERBS 23:7, KJV

When we believe we are declining, biology complies. When we believe we are renewing, biology complies.

Faith is not an escape from biology; it is its highest order. The Spirit does not bypass the body—it animates it.

THE STORIES THAT BIND US

Over the years, I have heard countless versions of the same story:

"I'd love to change, but it's my age."

"It's genetic."

"My metabolism slowed."

"This is just how my body is now."

I understand these narratives because I once lived inside them. They sound reasonable. But reason and reality are not the same.

These statements are not facts; they are instructions. Repeated often enough, they become agreements—and the body honors agreements faithfully.

Cells listen. The only question is what we are teaching them to believe.

FROM KNOWING TO BECOMING

Most people already know what to do. Information is not the barrier. Integration is.

The distance between knowledge and transformation is belief made embodied.

Dr. David Hamilton (2018) reminds us that every thought creates chemistry. Faith that remains intellectual produces little change. Faith that reaches the nervous system reshapes biology.

When belief becomes lived—felt, practiced, rehearsed—it becomes alignment. And alignment produces healing as a byproduct.

MY ONGOING PRACTICE

Even now, alignment is a daily discipline, not a permanent state.

Some mornings I wake up sore. At times, my reflection still hints at former identities—the soldier who pushed through pain, the skeptic who demanded proof, the man who once feared decline.

And then I remember: I have outgrown evidence before.

Pain once told me I was broken. Age once told me I was limited. Belief rewrote the story.

The practice now is not chasing health, but remembering wholeness.

Healing is not something I pursue. It is something I carry.

FAITH AS THE FINAL MEDICINE

If there is one truth I leave with you, let it be this:

Faith is not blind—it is biological.

When you align with the wholeness God placed within you, you activate the same intelligence that formed your body in the first place. The Spirit that authored your DNA has never forgotten how to heal it.

You are not waiting for a miracle. You are one in motion.

Every breath, every heartbeat, every act of gratitude and forgiveness is a sacred chemical event—a sermon written in flesh.

When you understand this, faith ceases to be effort and becomes essence. Health emerges not as a goal, but as a natural expression of remembrance.

LIVING THE INTEGRATION

To integrate mind, body, and spirit is to stop living in fragments.

It is to eat with gratitude. To move with awareness. To speak with faith. To rest without guilt.

It is to let your biology reflect your theology.

This is the lifelong path—not perfection, but presence. Not striving for health, but living as health.

Healing is not the reward of faith. Healing *is* faith—made visible.

FINAL REFLECTION

Tomorrow morning, when you stand before the mirror, do not search for evidence. Look for identity.

See beyond today's condition and recognize the design beneath it—divine intelligence, adaptability, and continual renewal.

Speak to that truth. Believe what God already knows:

You are whole.

Then live from that knowing until your body has no choice but to agree.

FROM UNDERSTANDING TO LIVING

This book was never meant to end with words alone.

Everything you've read—Scripture, science, story, and practice—points toward a single truth: healing becomes real when it is lived. Knowledge opens the door, but embodiment walks through it.

The sections that follow are not "extras," references, or academic add-ons. They are **tools for integration**—resources designed to support your practice, strengthen your confidence, and ground your faith in both evidence and experience.

Some readers will move slowly through them. Others will return often. There is no correct pace. Alignment unfolds uniquely for each person.

Think of these appendices not as assignments, but as **companions**—offered to you as reinforcement, reassurance, and renewal as you continue becoming whole.

APPENDIX A: THE SCIENCE BEHIND BELIEF, BIOLOGY, AND HEALING

Peer-Reviewed Research and Study Summaries

Faith does not require scientific validation—but for many, science removes unnecessary doubt.

This appendix gathers key peer-reviewed studies referenced throughout the book, offering a clear view of how belief, emotion, environment, and lifestyle influence physiology at the molecular, neurological, and systemic levels.

You do not need to read every study to benefit. Simply knowing that modern research consistently affirms what Scripture has long revealed can be deeply stabilizing. For some readers, this evidence provides intellectual peace; for others, it strengthens perseverance during seasons when progress feels subtle.

Use this section as reassurance, not proof. Healing does not depend on citation—but confidence often does.

APPENDIX B: PRACTICAL INTEGRATION AND DAILY ALIGNMENT

This appendix is where insight becomes habit.

Here you'll find distilled practices drawn from the chapters—simple, repeatable ways to align breath, belief, movement, emotion, and attention in daily life. These are not rigid protocols. They are **rhythms**, meant to adapt to your season, energy, and capacity.

Return to this section whenever alignment feels distant or fragmented. Even small, consistent practices restore coherence faster than intensity ever could.

Healing is rarely dramatic. It is cumulative. What you practice gently and faithfully becomes who you are.

APPENDIX C: RECOMMENDED READING AND STUDY RESOURCES FOR DEEP PRACTICE

Growth is not meant to stop here.

This appendix offers books, authors, and traditions that deepen the themes explored throughout the manuscript—neuroscience, epigenetics, spiritual formation, contemplative practice, and embodied faith.

These resources are not required reading. They are invitations. Follow curiosity, not obligation. Read what resonates. Leave what does not.

Truth multiplies when explored freely.

AUTHOR'S REFLECTIONS
A Final Word to the Reader

If there is one thing I hope you carry forward, it is this:

> You do not need to become someone new to heal. You
> need only to remember who you already are.

Every practice, every insight, every page of science or Scripture points back to that remembrance. Alignment is not something you achieve once—it is something you return to, again and again, with grace.

Thank you for walking this path with me.

PEER-REVIEWED RESEARCH AND STUDY SUMMARIES

The Science Behind Belief, Biology, and Healing

"Come now, and let us reason together, saith the Lord."
ISAIAH 1:18

OVERVIEW

This appendix provides brief summaries of scientific studies and peer-reviewed research supporting the mind–body connection, neuroplasticity, epigenetics, emotional coherence, and faith-based healing practices. Each summary highlights the key finding and its relevance to the themes explored in this book.

1. Psychoneuroimmunology—The Mind's Influence on Immunity

Pert, C. B. (1997). *Molecules of Emotion: The Science Behind Mind-Body Medicine.* Scribner.

Finding: Neurotransmitters once thought to exist only in the brain were discovered throughout the immune and endocrine systems.

Relevance: Every thought and emotion carries a biochemical signature that directly influences immune response. This discovery bridged psychology and physiology, showing that belief literally talks to biology.

Koenig, H. G. (2012). *The Healing Power of Faith.* Simon & Schuster.

Finding: Prayer and faith practices correlate with reduced stress hormones and improved cardiovascular and immune outcomes.

Relevance: Spiritual engagement activates measurable physiological healing responses.

2. Neuroplasticity—The Brain's Ability to Rewire

Doidge, N. (2007). *The Brain That Changes Itself.* Viking. https://normandoidge.com/

Finding: Repetition, focus, and intention can reorganize neural circuits even in adulthood.

Relevance: Mental rehearsal and visualization stimulate the same neural pathways as physical action—supporting the power of belief and imagery in recovery.

Decety, J. (1996). "The neurophysiological basis of motor imagery." *Behavioural Brain Research, 77*(1–2), 45–52.

Finding: Imagining movement activates nearly identical neural regions as performing it.

Relevance: Visualization is not fantasy; it is biological training.

3. Epigenetics—How Environment and Belief Shape Genes

Lipton, B. H. (2015). *The Biology of Belief: Unleashing the Power of Consciousness, Matter & Miracles.* Hay House. https://www.brucelipton.com/

Finding: Gene expression responds to perception and environment rather than fixed genetic code.

Relevance: Belief acts as a biochemical signal, turning healing genes on and off.

Meaney, M. J., & Szyf, M. (2005). "Environmental programming of stress responses through DNA methylation." *Dialogues in Clinical Neuroscience, 7*(2), 103–123.*

Finding: Early nurturing changes gene expression regulating stress in offspring.

Relevance: Emotional environment—care, safety, love—has lifelong biological consequences.

Ornish, D., et al. (2008). "Comprehensive lifestyle changes and telomerase activity." *The Lancet Oncology, 9*(11), 1020–1027.*

Finding: Diet, exercise, stress management, and social support lengthen telomeres.

Relevance: Conscious lifestyle and mindset directly influence cellular aging.

4. Meditation, Prayer, and Genetic Expression

Kaliman, P., et al. (2014). "Rapid changes in histone deacetylases and inflammatory gene expression in expert meditators." *Psychoneuroendocrinology, 40,* 96–107.*

Finding: Meditation alters gene expression tied to inflammation and immune regulation.

Relevance: Mental focus and gratitude create measurable biological change.

Bhasin, M. K., et al. (2013). "Relaxation response induces temporal transcriptome changes." *PLoS ONE, 8*(5), e62817.*

Finding: Relaxation and prayer practices regulate genes affecting metabolism and immune pathways.

Relevance: Spiritual calm isn't abstract—it's molecular.

5. Heart–Brain Coherence and Emotional Regulation

McCraty, R., Atkinson, M., & Bradley, R. T. (2009). "Electrophysiological evidence of intuition: Part 1." *Journal of Alternative and Complementary Medicine, 15*(2), 143–165.*

Finding: Feelings of love and gratitude produce coherent heart rhythms that synchronize with brain-wave patterns.

Relevance: Positive emotion aligns physiological systems, improving resilience and health.

Davidson, R. J., & McEwen, B. S. (2012). "Social influences on neuroplasticity." *Nature Neuroscience, 15*(5), 689–695.*

Finding: Compassion and mindfulness strengthen neural networks linked to well-being.

Relevance: Emotional coherence stabilizes biology.

6. The Placebo and Expectation Effect

Benedetti, F., et al. (2005). "Neurobiological mechanisms of the placebo effect." *Journal of Neuroscience, 25*(45), 10390–10402.*

Finding: Expectation alone triggers measurable dopamine, serotonin, and endorphin release.

Relevance: The body obeys belief—whether in medication or mindset.

Kaptchuk, T. J., et al. (2010). "Placebos without deception." *PLoS ONE, 5*(12), e15591.*

Finding: Even when participants know a pill is inert, healing still occurs if belief is engaged.

Relevance: Conscious expectation is a biological force.

7. Neurotheology and the Physiology of Faith

Newberg, A. B. (2018). *Neurotheology: How Science Can Enlighten Us About Spirituality.* Columbia University Press.

Finding: Prayer and worship alter neural activity in regions governing empathy, focus, and stress.

Relevance: Spiritual practice reshapes the brain toward peace and purpose.

8. Positive Emotion and Cellular Health

Fredrickson, B. L., et al. (2008). "Open hearts build lives." *Journal of Personality and Social Psychology, 95*(5), 1045–1062.*

Finding: Cultivating love and gratitude expands emotional resilience and immune function.

Relevance: Joy and compassion are regenerative biological states.

Blackburn, E. H., & Epel, E. S. (2017). *The Telomere Effect*. Grand Central Publishing.

Finding: Stress reduction and positive emotion preserve chromosomal telomere length.

Relevance: Peace of mind protects longevity.

CONCLUSION

Across every discipline—neuroscience, epigenetics, psychoneuroimmunology, and spirituality—the evidence converges: belief, emotion, and perception are not abstract experiences; they are biological directives.

Healing occurs when thought, feeling, and spirit speak the same language. Science describes the mechanism. Faith provides the meaning.

Together, they reveal this timeless truth: the power to heal has always lived within us.

SUPPLEMENTAL SOURCES
Integrative and Applied Perspectives
Wisdom is the bridge between knowledge and experience.

The following authors and works, while not peer-reviewed in the traditional academic sense, have contributed profoundly to the modern understanding of how consciousness, emotion, and faith shape physical reality. Their insights synthesize clinical observation, neuroscience, spirituality, and personal transformation. Each offers a living demonstration of the principles discussed throughout this book.

Dr. Joe Dispenza—The Neurobiology of Transformation

Key Works: *Becoming Supernatural: How Common People Are Doing the Uncommon* (2017)

Breaking the Habit of Being Yourself (2012)

Website: https://drjoedispenza.com/

Contribution: Dr. Dispenza blends neuroscience, epigenetics, and meditation practice to show how focused intention and elevated emotion rewire the brain and body. His workshops and case studies illustrate neuroplastic change, heart–brain coherence, and measurable healing outcomes among participants who align belief with emotion.

Relevance: Dispenza's work complements the principles of this book by translating laboratory findings into accessible daily disciplines of visualization, gratitude, and mental rehearsal.

Dr. David R. Hamilton—The Chemistry of Kindness

Key Work: *How Your Mind Can Heal Your Body* (2018) https://drdavidhamilton.com/

Contribution: Hamilton, a former pharmaceutical scientist, compiles peer-reviewed studies on the placebo effect, emotional chemistry, and compassionate physiology. He demonstrates that positive expectation, love, and belief alter immune function and gene expression.

Relevance: Hamilton serves as an interpreter between scientific literature and everyday life, making the biology of belief understandable and actionable for general readers.

Dr. Lynne Zimmerman—Integrative Healing in Practice

Key Work: *Heal Yourself: Using the Scientifically Proven Mind-Body Connection to Manage Chronic Pain, Depression, Cancer and More* (2012)

Contribution: Zimmerman synthesizes findings from psychoneuroimmunology, stress physiology, and energy medicine. Drawing on clinical experience, she presents practical tools for harnessing the body's innate healing mechanisms through awareness, relaxation, and spiritual connection.

Relevance: Her approach resonates with the core message of this book: that self-healing begins when consciousness becomes intentional and belief becomes embodied.

SYNTHESIS

Together, these thinkers expand the conversation from *knowing* to *doing*. They remind us that science describes the mechanism, but personal practice reveals the miracle. Their teachings echo the timeless truth that health is not granted from the outside—it is awakened from within.

PERSONAL REFLECTION—
LIVING THE INTEGRATION

In my own journey, these voices served as both compass and confirmation. When I began to explore how belief shapes biology, Dr. Hamilton offered the scientific grounding I needed, Dr. Zimmerman revealed how consciousness informs healing, and Dr. Dispenza demonstrated how daily practice turns knowledge into transformation. Their work gave language to what I was already living—the realization that faith is not an abstract virtue but a biological force.

By weaving their insights with scripture, hermetic philosophy, and lived experience, I came to see that every person carries the same capacity for renewal. We are not waiting for healing to arrive; we are remembering the truth that it already lives within us.

PRACTICAL INTEGRATION AND DAILY ALIGNMENT

"And be not conformed to this world: but be ye transformed by the renewing of your mind."

ROMANS 12:2, KJV

True healing is not achieved through knowledge alone but through practice. This appendix provides two complementary pathways:

Part 1 summarizes evidence-based mind-body protocols grounded in modern research.

Part 2 offers the 30-Day Belief Reset—a devotional routine for rewiring belief through daily repetition, reflection, and gratitude.

PART 1: SCIENCE-BACKED PRACTICES TO ACTIVATE THE MIND–BODY CONNECTION

1. Neuroplasticity and Visualization

(Doidge, 2007; Decety, 1996; Dispenza, 2017)

Practice—Mental Rehearsal: Spend 10 minutes daily imagining yourself moving, breathing, or healing with perfect ease. Visualize cellular repair, strong movement, and inner calm.

Protocol Tip: Pair visualization with slow, rhythmic breathing to synchronize neural and physiological patterns. Over time, these imagined actions become new neural blueprints for health and mobility.

2. Belief and Expectation

(Benedetti et al., 2005; Hamilton, 2018)

Practice—Positive Expectation Journaling: Each morning, record three positive expectations for your day: "My body is restoring balance." "I radiate energy and clarity." Each evening, reflect on progress or new sensations.

Protocol Tip: End journaling with two minutes of gratitude breathing to anchor belief in the nervous system. Expectation reshapes neurochemistry; your body follows the story you repeat.

3. Epigenetic and Emotional Alignment

(Lipton, 2015; Meaney & Szyf, 2005; Ornish et al., 2008)

Practice—Environmental and Emotional Coherence: Simplify your environment: declutter, open light, surround yourself with music and color that uplift. Nurture emotional coherence through daily gratitude, forgiveness, and mindful compassion.

Protocol Tip: Observe physical changes when you shift emotional tone. Love, joy, and safety signal your genes to repair; fear and stress tell them to defend.

4. Heart–Brain Coherence and Spiritual Alignment

(McCraty et al., 2009; Koenig, 2012; Zimmerman, 2012)

Practice—Heart-Focused Breathing & Prayer: Sit comfortably, hand on heart. Inhale 5 counts, exhale 5 counts while focusing on gratitude or love. Transition into prayer or reflection, feeling peace radiate outward.

Protocol Tip: Use this before stressful events or workouts to activate parasympathetic balance. Faith and physiology share the same rhythm when gratitude leads the breath.

5. Mindful Presence and Positive Emotion
(Fredrickson et al., 2008; Davidson & Kabat-Zinn, 2003; Langer, 2014)

Practice—Joy and Gratitude Expansion: Notice beauty and small victories throughout your day. Record three moments of gratitude each evening and relive them with feeling.

Protocol Tip: Positive emotion widens perception, enhances immunity, and anchors the biology of peace. As scripture affirms, "A merry heart doeth good like a medicine: but a broken spirit drieth the bones." (Proverbs 17:22)

IMPLEMENTATION FRAMEWORK

Time	Practice	Focus
Morning	Gratitude journaling + visualization	Set expectation for healing
Midday	Emotion check-in + mindful movement	Sustain awareness and calm
Evening	Reflection + heart-focused breathing	Integrate peace before rest

Even five intentional minutes, repeated daily, create lasting neural and cellular change.

PART 2: THE 30-DAY BELIEF RESET— TRAINING THE INNER ENVIRONMENT

Healing begins when thought, feeling, and faith align. This 30-Day practice is designed to retrain perception and establish coherence between mind, body, and spirit.

How to Use

1. Create Space: Practice upon waking and before sleep.
2. Speak Aloud: Declare each line slowly until you feel it.
3. Visualize Wholeness: Imagine yourself already whole.
4. Reflect and Record: Note sensations or insights.
5. Repeat for 30 Days: Consistency rewires belief into biology.

READER'S DAILY AFFIRMATION— "I AM WHOLENESS IN MOTION"

Morning Declaration

Today, I choose alignment.

My mind, body, and spirit move as one.

Every cell in me responds to peace.

Every thought I think shapes my healing.

I am not the sum of my past or my pain.

I am the expression of divine intelligence.

Where others see limitation, I see opportunity.

Where fear speaks, I answer with faith.

I am being renewed moment by moment.

Healing flows through me effortlessly.

I do not wait for miracles—

I live as one.

Evening Reflection

As I rest, my body restores itself.

Every breath brings renewal.

Every heartbeat affirms life.

I release all doubt, resistance, and comparison.

My body listens to my belief.

My mind agrees with truth.

My spirit anchors me in peace.

I am whole.

I am healed.

I am home within myself.

REFLECTION PROMPTS

Morning:

- What truth will I embody today?

- How can I align my thoughts with gratitude?

Evening:

- Where did I feel peace or resistance?

- What will I release before rest?

30-DAY PRACTICE TRACKER

Day	Morning	Evening	Notes / Insights
1			
2			
3			
4			
5			
6			
7			
8			
9			
10			
11			
12			
13			
14			
15			

16			
17			
18			
19			
20			
21			
22			
23			
24			
25			
26			
27			
28			
29			
30			

CLOSING GUIDANCE

This reset is not a ritual of striving but of remembering. Each repetition tells your cells that peace is safe, wholeness is normal, and healing is the body's native state.

At the end of thirty days, you will not merely think differently—you will *be* different. Your mind will think in faith, your body will act in coherence, and your spirit will rest in certainty.

The science describes *how*; belief reveals *why*. Together, they restore the whole.

RECOMMENDED READING AND STUDY RESOURCES FOR DEEP PRACTICE

"With all thy getting, get understanding."
PROVERBS 4:7

Healing is both revelation and discipline. The following works are offered as companions, not replacements, to *Getting Healthy from the Inside Out: Harnessing the Power of Belief, Mindset, and Faith.* Each selection deepens the conversation at the intersection of science, spirit, psychology, and embodied practice, inviting continued growth long after the final page.

These texts were chosen for their intellectual rigor, spiritual resonance, and practical applicability. Together, they form a coherent body of study for those committed to lifelong alignment.

1. The Science of Belief, Consciousness, and Neuroplasticity

Lipton, Bruce H. (2015). *The Biology of Belief.* Hay House. A foundational work in epigenetics demonstrating how perception and environment regulate genetic expression.

Website: https://www.brucelipton.com/

Hamilton, David R. (2018). *How Your Mind Can Heal Your Body.* Hay House. Bridges psychoneuroimmunology and compassion science, translating research into daily practice.

Website: https://drdavidhamilton.com/

Dispenza, Joe. (2017). *Becoming Supernatural.* Hay House. Explores neuroplasticity, meditation, and belief as mechanisms for measurable biological change.

Website: https://drjoedispenza.com/

Siegel, Daniel J. (2010). *Mindsight: The New Science of Personal Transformation.* Bantam. Introduces integrative neuroscience, showing how awareness reshapes the brain toward coherence and health.

Website: https://drdansiegel.com/

2. Mind–Body Medicine and Emotional Integration

Maté, Gabor. (2003). *When the Body Says No.* Knopf Canada. Examines the relationship between suppressed emotion, chronic stress, and disease.

Website: https://drgabormate.com/

Ornish, Dean, & Ornish, Anne. (2019). *Undo It!.* Ballantine Books. Demonstrates how lifestyle medicine—combined with meaning and connection—can reverse chronic illness. *Website:* https://www.ornish.com/

Pert, Candace B. (1997). *Molecules of Emotion.* Scribner. A seminal text revealing how emotions function as biochemical messengers throughout the body.

Davidson, Richard J., & Kabat-Zinn, Jon. (2003). "Alterations in Brain and Immune Function Produced by Mindfulness Meditation."

Psychosomatic Medicine, 65(4), 564–570.* Landmark research connecting contemplative practice to immune and neurological change.

3. Spirituality, Scripture, and the Healing Tradition

Koenig, Harold G. (2012). *The Healing Power of Faith*. Simon & Schuster. A comprehensive scientific review of prayer, spirituality, and health outcomes.

Goddard, Neville. (1948). *Feeling Is the Secret*. DeVorss & Company. A concise spiritual text emphasizing imagination and emotion as creative forces.

The Holy Bible—with particular attention to: Proverbs 4:23; Romans 12:2; Mark 5:34; Philippians 4:8 Scriptural foundations for the renewal of mind, heart, and embodied faith.

Three Initiates. (1908). *The Kybalion*. Introduces Hermetic principles—mentalism, vibration, correspondence—that prefigure modern consciousness theory.

4. Psychology, Identity, and Behavioral Change

Bandura, Albert. (1997). *Self-Efficacy: The Exercise of Control*. W. H. Freeman. Establishes belief in one's capability as a primary determinant of performance and resilience.

Beck, Aaron T. (2011). *Cognitive Therapy of Depression*. Guilford Press. The clinical foundation for cognitive restructuring and identity-based change.

Clear, James. (2018). *Atomic Habits*. Avery. A modern, evidence-based framework for how small, consistent actions shape identity and long-term outcomes. *Especially valuable for translating belief into daily embodiment.* *https://jamesclear.com/*

Duhigg, Charles. (2012). *The Power of Habit*. Random House. Explores the neurological loops that govern behavior and habit formation.

Website: https://charlesduhigg.com/

Fredrickson, Barbara L. (2009). *Positivity*. Crown. Demonstrates how gratitude and joy expand cognitive, emotional, and physiological capacity.

Website: https://www.pursuit-of-happiness.org/

5. Energy, Coherence, and Heart Intelligence

McCraty, Rollin. (2017). *Science of the Heart*. HeartMath Institute. Presents research on heart–brain coherence and its effects on emotional regulation and health.

Website: https://www.heartmath.org/

Levin, Jeff. (2001). *God, Faith, and Health*. John Wiley & Sons. A global survey of epidemiological research on spirituality and well-being.

Website: http://religionandhealth.com/

Rubik, Beverly. (2002). "The Biofield Hypothesis." *Journal of Alternative and Complementary Medicine, 8*(6), 703–717.* Explores the body's electromagnetic communication system as a potential healing interface.

6. Purpose, Meaning, and Lifelong Integration

Newberg, Andrew B. (2018). *Neurotheology*. Columbia University Press. Examines how spiritual practice reshapes the brain and emotional regulation.

Blackburn, Elizabeth H., & Epel, Elissa S. (2017). *The Telomere Effect.* Grand Central Publishing. Links stress, mindset, and meaning to cellular aging and longevity.

Zimmerman, Lynne. (2012). *Heal Yourself.* Watkins Publishing. Integrates mind–body practices for chronic pain, illness, and emotional healing.

Frankl, Viktor E. (1946). *Man's Search for Meaning.* Beacon Press. A timeless exploration of purpose as the deepest determinant of survival and vitality.

SUGGESTED APPROACH TO STUDY

- **Read for Integration, Not Accumulation.** Look for patterns that unite belief, biology, and spirit rather than isolated techniques.

- **Pair Learning with Embodiment.** Translate insight into practice through journaling, prayer, movement, or stillness.

- **Study in Community.** Shared reflection deepens understanding and reinforces coherence.

- **Return Often to Scripture and Silence.** Knowledge matures into wisdom only when anchored in presence.

FINAL REFLECTION

Learning becomes sacred when it leads to transformation. The voices represented here—scientists, physicians, mystics, and teachers—speak a single truth in many dialects:

The body becomes what the mind believes.

Let these works guide you deeper into daily alignment, where knowledge ripens into knowing, belief becomes biology, and faith is lived—not merely held.

BIBLIOGRAPHY

SOURCES AND FURTHER READING

The works listed here did not enter my life all at once, nor for academic reasons alone. Each appeared at a particular moment—often when I was searching for understanding, relief, or language for what I was experiencing in my own body and faith. Some challenged long-held assumptions. Others offered clarity when clarity was scarce. Together, they shaped the way I learned to see health, belief, and healing from the inside out.

This book is not a summary of these sources, nor an endorsement of every conclusion they present. It is the integration that emerged after these ideas were lived, tested, and carried through seasons of uncertainty, recovery, and growth. What remains is what proved true—not only on the page, but in practice.

Ader, R., Cohen, N., & Felten, D. (1995). Psychoneuroimmunology: Interactions between the nervous system and the immune system. *The Lancet*, 345(8942), 99–103.

Afshin, A., et al. (2019). Health effects of dietary risks in 195 countries, 1990–2017. *The Lancet*, 393(10184), 1958–1972.

Bandura, A. (1997). *Self-efficacy: The exercise of control.* W. H. Freeman.

Beck, A. T. (2011). *Cognitive therapy of depression.* Guilford Press.

Beecher, H. K. (1955). The powerful placebo. *Journal of the American Medical Association*, 159(17), 1602–1606.

Benedetti, F. (2014). *Placebo effects: Understanding the mechanisms in health and disease.* Oxford University Press.

Benedetti, F., Mayberg, H. S., Wager, T. D., Stohler, C. S., & Zubieta, J.-K. (2005). Neurobiological mechanisms of the placebo effect. *Journal of Neuroscience*, 25(45), 10390–10402.

Bhasin, M. K., et al. (2013). Relaxation response induces temporal transcriptome changes in energy metabolism, insulin secretion, and inflammatory pathways. *PLoS ONE*, 8(5), e62817.

Buddharakkhita, A. (Trans.). (1985). *The Dhammapada.* Buddhist Publication Society. (Original work composed c. 3rd century BCE)

Cappuccio, F. P., et al. (2010). Sleep duration and all-cause mortality. *Sleep*, 33(5), 585–592.

Clear, J. (2018). *Atomic habits.* Avery.

Cohen, S., Janicki-Deverts, D., & Miller, G. E. (2007). Psychological stress and disease. *Journal of the American Medical Association*, 298(14), 1685–1687.

Cohen, S., et al. (2012). Social relationships and health. *American Psychologist*, 59(8), 676–684.

Creswell, J. D., et al. (2022). Mindfulness interventions and inflammatory biology. *Psychiatry Research*, 311, 114492.

Crichton, F., et al. (2015). The placebo effect and pain modulation. *Psychosomatic Medicine*, 77(5), 552–561.

Csikszentmihályi, M. (1990). *Flow: The psychology of optimal experience.* Harper & Row.

Czeisler, C. A. (2013). Perspective: Casting light on sleep deficiency. *Nature, 497,* S13.

Davidson, R. J., & McEwen, B. S. (2012). Social influences on neuroplasticity. *Nature Neuroscience, 15*(5), 689–695.

Decety, J. (1996). Neural representations for motor imagery. *Behavioural Brain Research, 77*(1–2), 45–52.

Dispenza, J. (2014). *You are the placebo: Making your mind matter.* Hay House.

Dispenza, J. (2017). *Breaking the habit of being yourself.* Hay House.

Dispenza, J. (2019). *Becoming supernatural: How common people are doing the uncommon.* Hay House.

Doidge, N. (2007). *The brain that changes itself.* Viking.

Duhigg, C. (2012). *The power of habit.* Random House.

Epel, E. S., & Blackburn, E. H. (2017). *The telomere effect.* Grand Central Publishing.

Frankl, V. E. (1946/2006). *Man's search for meaning.* Beacon Press.

Fredrickson, B. L., et al. (2008). Open hearts build lives. *Journal of Personality and Social Psychology, 95*(5), 1045–1062.

Galante, J., et al. (2014). Effect of meditation on inflammatory gene expression. *Psychoneuroendocrinology, 42,* 123–130.

Gotink, R. A., et al. (2023). Meditation and neuroplasticity: A meta-analysis. *Neuroscience & Biobehavioral Reviews, 145,* 105024.

Gupta, A., et al. (2024). Heart-rate variability and cognitive resilience. *Frontiers in Neuroscience*, 18, 129874.

Hamilton, D. R. (2018). *How your mind can heal your body* (2nd ed.). Hay House.

Harvey, P. (2013). *An introduction to Buddhism: Teachings, history and practices* (2nd ed.). Cambridge University Press.

HeartMath Institute. (2017). *Science of the heart* (2nd ed.). HeartMath.

Jirtle, R. L., & Skinner, M. K. (2007). Environmental epigenomics. *Nature Reviews Genetics*, 8(4), 253–262.

Kaliman, P., et al. (2014). Rapid changes in gene expression following meditation. *Psychoneuroendocrinology*, 40, 96–107.

Kaptchuk, T. J., et al. (2010). Placebos without deception. *PLoS ONE*, 5(12), e15591.

Koenig, H. G. (2012). *The healing power of faith*. Simon & Schuster.

Kühn, S., et al. (2014). Silence and the brain. *Brain Structure and Function*, 219(6), 1865–1871.

Langer, E. J. (2009). *Counterclockwise: Mindful health and the power of possibility*. Ballantine Books.

Lear, S. A., et al. (2017). Physical activity and mortality. *The Lancet*, 390(10113), 2643–2654.

Lin, Y., et al. (2023). EEG–ECG coherence and emotional regulation. *Frontiers in Human Neuroscience*, 17, 118734.

Lipton, B. H. (2005). *The biology of belief*. Hay House.

Lipton, B. H. (2015). *The honeymoon effect*. Hay House.

Longo, V. D., & Panda, S. (2016). Fasting, circadian rhythms, and healthspan. *Cell Metabolism*, 23(6), 1048–1059.

Maté, G. (2003). *When the body says no*. Knopf Canada.

McCraty, R., Atkinson, M., Tomasino, D., & Bradley, R. T. (2009). The coherent heart. *Global Advances in Health and Medicine*, 8(1), 10–38.

McEwen, B. S., & Wingfield, J. C. (2010). Allostasis and health. *Hormones and Behavior*, 57(2), 105–111.

Meaney, M. J., & Szyf, M. (2005). Maternal care and epigenetic programming. *Trends in Neurosciences*, 28(9), 456–463.

Newberg, A. (2018). *Neurotheology: How science can enlighten us about spirituality*. Columbia University Press.

Ornish, D. (2008). Lifestyle changes and gene expression. *Proceedings of the National Academy of Sciences*, 105(24), 8369–8374.

Post, S. G. (2005). Altruism and health. *International Journal of Behavioral Medicine*, 12(2), 66–77.

Ruiz, J. R., et al. (2008). Muscular strength and mortality. *British Medical Journal*, 337, a439.

Siegel, D. J. (2010). *Mindsight*. Bantam.

Shonkoff, J. P., et al. (2012). The lifelong effects of early childhood adversity. *Pediatrics*, 129(1), e232–e246.

Three Initiates. (1908/2011). *The Kybalion*. Tarcher.

U.S. Army. (2025). *Master Resilience Training: Historical overview and program transition memorandum*.

Department of the Army.

Zimmerman, L. (2020). Identity, belief, and biological regulation. *Journal of Mind-Body Health*, 14(3), 201–219.

THE JOURNEY FROM DIAGNOSIS TO WHOLENESS

I am a retired Army soldier with more than three decades of service. Like most who spend that long in uniform, I didn't leave the Army untouched. I left with scars, chronic pain, and a medical record thick enough to tell a very convincing story about why my best days were behind me.

Nothing life-threatening—but plenty painful.

Surgeries. Degenerative joints. Disc issues. Nerve damage. Tinnitus that never takes a day off. Along the way came diagnoses including Major Depressive Disorder with anxious distress and a Traumatic Brain Injury. Each diagnosis was supported by imaging, tests, and expert opinion. The evidence was overwhelming—and I believed every bit of it.

Many of my peers retired with similar records. Some proudly displayed disabled plates and placards—clear markers of identity. No judgment. They earned them.

I chose a different path.

I didn't deny the pain, but I refused to let a diagnosis become who

I was. I didn't want my future defined solely by what had been damaged. I wanted to believe—perhaps stubbornly—that I was still whole.

While working on my doctoral degree, I gained access to the research that underpins this book. I wasn't searching for inspiration; I was searching for consistency. I compared neuroscience, psychology, epigenetics, theology, and ancient philosophy. I followed Dr. Joe Dispenza. I studied scripture with renewed intention. I explored the *Kybalion* and other metaphysical texts—not for escape, but for pattern recognition.

What surprised me wasn't how different these disciplines were—it was how often they pointed to the same conclusion: healing begins within.

That idea was uncomfortable at first. It meant I could no longer rely solely on external explanations. I had to examine belief itself— how much authority I had given to labels, prognoses, and expectations.

I'm deeply grateful to my wife for introducing me to Neville Goddard. That encounter shifted my understanding of God—not as distant or abstract, but as the designer of a body built for adaptation and repair when placed in the right environment. And belief, I came to realize, is part of that environment.

Gradually, something changed. I began healing faster. Pain resolved more efficiently. Injuries that once lingered moved through me instead of settling in. Not dramatically. Not instantly. But consistently.

This was not magic. It was a process—learned, practiced, and refined. It required discipline, persistence, faith, and more patience than I would have preferred. Some days showed progress. Others reminded me that healing is rarely linear.

To be clear, this is not a rejection of medicine. I still respect medical care and intervention when appropriate. This is not rebellion—it's relationship. Medicine became a tool, not an identity. Belief became the foundation.

I no longer begin with what the records say. I begin with what I know to be true: the body is intelligent, adaptive, and responsive. Given the right internal and external environment, it moves toward healing.

This path isn't fast. It isn't flashy. It doesn't promise perfection.

But it works.

And if someone with decades of documented injuries and diagnoses can move toward wholeness—not perfection, but wholeness—then perhaps health isn't about fixing what's broken after all.

Perhaps it's about remembering what was never truly lost.

A FINAL WORD TO THE READER

If there is one truth I hope you carry from these pages, it is this: you are not broken. You were never created defective, and you are not at the mercy of your past, your diagnosis, or your DNA. The same intelligence that formed your body from a single cell continues to operate within you right now—ready to restore, renew, and regenerate in ways that often defy logic but never defy divine law.

Healing begins the moment you believe it's possible. The shift does not start in a doctor's office, a pill bottle, or a fitness plan—it starts in the invisible space of your own awareness. It begins when you stop asking, *"What's wrong with me?"* and begin declaring, *"What's right with me?"*

This journey will require faith. Not blind faith, but a faith informed by understanding—a faith that blends the wisdom of scripture, the revelations of science, and the timeless principles of spiritual truth. It will require patience, persistence, and courage to see beyond what the world calls "evidence." But in time, as your inner belief reshapes your biology, you will witness what Jesus meant when He said, *"According to your faith be it unto you."*

To those who have carried pain, to those who have been told their bodies cannot heal, to those who have given up on hope—I offer my story as living proof that transformation is possible. Not because I am special, but because I finally stopped believing in limitations.

May this book be both a map and a mirror. A map to guide you back to alignment with the truth of who you are—and a mirror that reflects the divine wholeness that has been within you all along.

Your healing has already begun. Believe it, and your body will follow.

ACKNOWLEDGMENTS

This book is the culmination of years of seeking, questioning, and learning—but more than anything, it is the fruit of faith, love, and divine guidance expressed through the people who have walked beside me on this journey.

To my wonderful wife, Melissa—thank you for being both my anchor and my inspiration. Your unwavering belief in me has been a living example of what unconditional love looks like in practice. You were the one who first introduced me to Neville Goddard, opening the door to a deeper understanding of imagination, faith, and creation itself. Your patience, wisdom, and quiet strength have sustained me through every stage of this transformation.

To my spiritual teachers and scientific influences—Dr. Joe Dispenza, Dr, Gabor Maté, Dr. David R. Hamilton, Dr. Bruce Lipton, Dr. Lynne Zimmerman, Dr. Ellen Langer, Neville Goddard, and so many others who have devoted their lives to bridging the gap between science and spirit—thank you for showing that the miraculous is not an anomaly, but the blueprint of creation. Your courage to explore the unknown continues to inspire both my mind and my faith.

To the medical professionals who had the courage to tell me that healing was possible—even when evidence said otherwise—thank you. You reminded me that medicine, at its best, is not defined by technology or prescription, but by compassion, curiosity, and a belief in the body's divine intelligence.

To the readers who instinctively know that Western medicine alone is not the full story—this book was written for you. For those who have tried, prayed, and persisted without seeing results, may these pages offer you a bridge between knowledge and belief, a path of integration, and the realization that your body is not your adversary, but your most sacred ally.

To my Bible study group, who have graciously tolerated—and often encouraged—my "outlandish" questions about faith, consciousness, and the mysteries of God, thank you for allowing me to wrestle with truth and reverence in equal measure. Your fellowship reminds me that real faith is not brittle—it grows stronger through inquiry.

And finally, to the many teachers, mentors, and fellow seekers I've met along the way—those who walk with humility, live with wonder, and dare to believe that we are more than flesh and bone—thank you. Each of you has added a brushstroke to this greater picture of divine wholeness.

To all who read these words: may you come to know that the power to heal has always been within you. My deepest gratitude goes to you for walking this path of remembrance with me.

www.ingramcontent.com/pod-product-compliance
Lightning Source LLC
Chambersburg PA
CBHW031046160726
47991CB00005B/2044